TRAVELS IN THE SKIN TRADE

Tourism and the Sex Industry

JEREMY SEABROOK

Pluto Press
LONDON • CHICAGO, IL.

First published 1996 by Pluto Press
345 Archway Road, London N6 5AA
and 1436 West Randolph, Chicago, IL 60607, USA

British Library Cataloguing in Publication Data
A catalogue record for this book is available from
the British Library

ISBN 0 7453 1115 6 hbk

Library of Congress Cataloging in Publication Data
Seabrook, Jeremy, 1939–
Travels in the skin trade : tourism and the sex industry /
Jeremy Seabrook.
p.   cm.
ISBN 0–7453–1115–6 (hbk)
1. Sex oriented businesses—Thailand—Bangkok.
2. Sex tourism—Thailand—Bangkok.   I. Title.
HQ242.55.B3S43   1996
306.74'09593—dc20   96–34398
CIP

Printing history:
99 98 97 96   4 3 2 1

Designed, typeset and produced for Pluto Press by
Chase Production Services, Chipping Norton
Printed in the EC by J.W. Arrowsmith Ltd, Bristol

Contents

Foreword

SIRIPORN SKROBANEK
Foundation for Women, Bangkok

Women in the sex industry in Thailand have been for a long time the object of international investigation, both by Western scholars and media people. Through their studies and reports, women in Thailand are viewed as 'the other women', whose status is perceived as lower than that of women in the West. Moral judgements, paternalistic attitudes towards Thai society in general, and Thai women in particular, are commonplace when one reads publications on this subject. Certainly there are elements in Thai society which contribute to the growth of commercialisation of human relationships, both in the family and community, and to the commodification of women's body and soul. But since there are two sides in a commercial transaction between foreign visitors and Thai women, why is only one party to the deal (Thai women and their society) the target of investigation, while the other party (the sex tourists) goes unexamined? It is more difficult to look into one's own heart than to impose one's own moral judgement on the people and culture of others.

Jeremy Seabrook is among the few who have accepted this challenge, and has painstakingly searched the soul of his fellow men, their motives and expectations in coming to the land of smiles. We learn from his research that they are not a homogeneous group, and from their own words, one can see a range of characters, from a heartbreaking man who needs to be pampered to a white master who wants to conquer.

The book is, therefore, not only about a sex industry in Thailand, but also a reflection of a human tragedy. Thailand is like a stage, where men from around the world come to perform their role of male supremacy over Thai women, and their white supremacy over Thai people. Through their own words, we see they do not want to learn about the people and culture, they just want to exploit the natural beauty and the female body.

The women in this book are not naive innocents, but human beings, capable of taking control of their life. They know how to play in this power game, where men want to dominate and are ready to place blame on anyone but themselves when things go wrong, or when anyone challenges their supremacy. As a Thai woman, it was painful to read between the lines, seeing the transactions in this 'virtual love', which ends so often in contempt and violence by the foreign men against Thai women. Many such relationships are nothing but a social pathology which they do not perceive. They tend to continue to divide women between the two cultures as 'the one who taught me to hate and the other who taught me to cry'.

Among all the exploitation and misunderstanding, however, Seabrook also shows us some more tender relationships between men and Thai women. Nevertheless, the question still arises: to what extent can such a relationship survive, based as it is on the man's naivete and the woman's survival strategy?

Another problem with prostitution in Thailand is that Western men need more than sexual services from Thai sex workers. They look for loving care, sincerity and honesty, which are not part of this power game and which they certainly do not expect in their home countries. The blame is again placed on the Thai women, who dare to make them realise the reality of the prostitution business.

Unlike other literature on this subject, Seabrook's work also voices the concerns and actions of various organisations and individuals working to ameliorate the problem of sex tourism, as well as to help women and children involved in the sex industry. From their own accounts, one can see that many Thai activists, female and male, have, in their various ways, the dream of a struggle to stop sexual exploitation of children and women in Thailand.

They link the sexual exploitation to the unjust and unequal structural relationships between rich and poor, man and woman, and between countries. They are also in search of a new development paradigm, as they realise that the existing one has devoured human relationships and spiritual dignity, and is making us all slaves of modern consumerism.

Seabrook has contributed to the study of the sex industry in Thailand. He has completed the jigsaw which allows us to see a fuller picture, not only of the sex industry of Thailand, but also of the increasingly instrumental nature of relationships between people in the West. The solution to international sexual exploitation lies, not only in changing the commercialised pattern of relationships in Thailand, but also those between the people of the West itself; for the sake of liberation, both for the exploited of Thailand, and for the whole of humanity.

Bangkok, July 1996

PREFACE

This book is about the sex industry in Bangkok, the men who go there, the young women (and young men and children) who service them, the growing 'market' for sexual partners, and the people who are both resisting the sex trade and working to empower those within it. But it is also about human rights – some of them scarcely contentious, such as the rights of women and children not to be trafficked as commodities and not to be compelled or duped into prostitution, the right not to be abused or brutalised by the military or the forces of law and order.

It also raises the question of other rights which are more disputed, such as, for instance, the rights of rich males to get on an aircraft and travel across the world in order to exercise the power of their money over others. These infringements of the rights of others may be less obvious than the more overt brutalities of repression by governments, but they can be equally damaging to those on the receiving end of the actions of the powerful and to those who must live – or die – with the consequences.

Last but not least, the question of economic rights is addressed – the right to livelihood, the right to secure employment, the right not to depend upon prostitution as the only form of labour open to women. For all the civil and political rights which the West – quite properly – defends rest upon a more fundamental right, the right to life itself; without the right to grow peacefully, free from want and destitution which lead to malnutrition, avoidable illness and premature death, all other rights are cancelled.

In this way, the book argues for a more ample and gener-ous interpretation of human rights than those presently acknowledged by the West. It does so by presenting the expe-riences and first-hand accounts of a wide section of those involved in the sex industry in Bangkok – clients, customers, women, children, activists, academics. It also contains sug-gestions for those who would like to help in the efforts and campaigns against the abuse of young women, men and chil-dren – particularly those presently being conducted by End Child Prostitution in Asian Tourism (ECPAT) and the Coali-tion Against Child Prostitution in the United Kingdom.

I have drawn upon the work of many people working with and on behalf of the sex workers of Thailand. I would like to make special mention of Riyoko Michinobu, whose unpub-lished thesis contains much useful historical material, of San-phosit Koompraphant, Chris Macmahon of the Centre for the Protection of Children's Rights in Bangkok; I have quoted from *A Modern Form of Slavery*, published by the Asia Watch and Women's Rights Project. I am indebted for their insights and helpful contribution to Chantawipa Apisuk of EMPOWER, Siriporn Skrobanek of the Foundation for Women, Thanavadee Thajen of the Friends of Women, Sudarat Srisang of FACE and the members of End Child Prostitution in Asian Tourism. I had originally compiled the interviews with male visitors to Bangkok for the Women's Groups and non-governmental organisations (NGOs), as material that will illuminate for them something of the motives and the psyche of Western clients of sex workers in Thailand.

I would like to thank Julia O'Connell-Davidson and Jacqueline Marquez-Taylor of the University of Leicester for their work on sex tourism in the Caribbean and South America as well as Asia. I am grateful to Julia for her helpful criticism of the manuscript. I would like to acknowledge Anne Badger and Helen Veitch of the Coalition Against Child Prostitution, and give warmest thanks to Margaret Lynch and her colleagues at War on Want for their support and encouragement.

Jeremy Seabrook
Bangkok/London
June 1996

1

SEX AS INDUSTRY

The sex industry of Bangkok is conspicuous, but embraces only a very small fraction of the population. The great majority of the people of Bangkok are employed in industry and construction, in workshops and factories, in hotels, shops, in the provision of food from street stalls and restaurants, in transport and tourism, in commerce, trade, in offices, in the law and education. There are scores of thousands of young women in the garments industry. Many of them work up to 15 or 16 hours a day; they live, eat and sleep in the 'row-house' factories where they work. They regularly send money home to their families and whole villages are sustained by their remittances. In shared rooms, photographs of their parents, brothers and sisters keep memories of home alive; a battered suitcase, some clothes, a mat for sleeping. Some, no doubt, find their way into the more lucrative employment of the the bars or clubs, especially if a friend or acquaintance introduces them to it; but most women in the city remain untouched by the sex industry. The reputation of Bangkok as a sort of global brothel is both unjust and untrue.

In the last three years, I have spent many months in Bangkok, originally looking at migration, industrial workers and the process of urbanisation. Between September 1995 and March 1996 however, I concentrated more closely on the 'demand' side of the sex trade, at least in so far as this involves Western visitors, residents and tourists in the city. These categories are not always easy to distinguish and they merge into each other. Many who visit Thailand for the melancholy kind of 'fun' for which Bangkok has a somewhat exaggerated reputation, find they get hooked; or maybe enchanted. Many are drawn to come again and again. Some settle in Thailand, more or less permanently: sexpatriates.

The interactions reflected here address, for the most part, the longer-term involvement between Thais and Westerners, although there are accounts of more casual, transient visitors too. The contacts were made in a variety of ways – some through friends and acquaintances, some as direct interviews; but mainly, as encounters in bars, public places and clubs, often informally.

It is important to be aware of the limitations of such methods. For one thing, people are usually more ready to talk – particularly to strangers – about the breakdown of relationships, to dwell upon the causes of emotional and cultural incomprehension between Thai and foreigner, than they are to discuss successful, long-term attachments: these tend to celebrate themselves quietly, privately and rarely become the object of the same kind of morose introspection which follows separation or break-up. People who are disappointed or who feel that they have been deceived are more likely to express their frustrations. In that sense, these meetings and encounters cannot be said to be 'representative'. But in an attempt to reach some insight into the motives, responses and attitudes of foreign men in Bangkok, I have set out what I gained from 20 or so meetings in late 1995 and early 1996. These are mostly with Westerners (for linguistic reasons, it was not possible to speak with Japanese or Taiwanese, etc. although I did meet one or two Indians).

Some of these encounters are immensely touching: some illuminating, others pitiable, even repelling. The book does concentrate on the 'demand' side, because I wanted to discover what it is about the rich and envied societies of the West that impels so many people to travel across the world to look for experiences which are, presumably, not available to them at home. If I wanted to defend sex tourism – and there is no shortage of evidence on which to condemn it – I would perhaps quote the elderly American who said that he had never been touched by another human being for more than a quarter of a century until he came to Bangkok. When I quoted this example to some women in Britain, their response was 'Why couldn't he go to American sex workers?' They have a point, of course. The whole story of travelling abroad for sex implies that you can do things with foreigners that you cannot do at home, which is a racist assumption.

But it is also true that, on the whole, Western sex workers do not regard the giving of affection as part of the deal; and this distinction is less readily made in parts of the South.

The stories the people tell reveal something of the transactions between farangs (foreigners) and young Thai women and men. One of the original reasons for writing this book was to help Thai sex workers cope with the mysterious West, in the same way that those people who come to Thailand need to know much more than they do about the destination they choose; their fascination with an East, which frequently withholds its secrets, leaves them baffled and sometimes angry. The men who narrate their stories in this book are not representative of sex tourists: they are, for the most part, regular vistors to, or residents in, Thailand. This makes them untypical, but may have the advantage of explaining deeper Western responses and attitudes towards Thai women than the views of short-term sex tourists.

One thing that clearly draws Western men to Thai women is the perceived capacity of the women for what I can only describe as tenderness; a quality conspicuously absent from the sex industry in the West. Men feel particularly cherished by what they experience as the compliance, eagerness to please and considerateness of Thai women. Many compared such responses very favourably with the more mechanistic and functional behaviour of most Western sex workers. Just how far they are responding to an unchallenged indulgence in the power their money secures for them becomes clearer through their own words.

There is a pattern in the relationships between Thai women and foreigners who return again and again to Thailand. In the early stages of their contact with Thai women, the men tend to express the delight that comes from revelation – they describe themselves as being over the moon, being on cloud nine, walking on air and wondered what they have been doing, wasting their life until now. They rarely see that this idealisation of 'Oriental' women is as racist as the subsequent disillusionment. It is easy for them to forget, as Beth of EMPOWER (an NGO devoted to enabling sex workers to achieve greater equality with their clients, by teaching them their legal rights and health education, as well as providing language classes that help them negotiate with

foreigners) puts it, that 'these are working women, for God's
sake'. And what is more, they are working women with
families to support. When Westerners, who have become the
lovers of sex workers, discover this, they frequently become
angry and claim they have been cheated. It is then that
overtly racist responses – which are, of course, present in the
whole activity of sex tourism – become explicit. It is very
difficult for people from the West to understand emotionally
(however clear their intellectual recognition may be) that the
family is the sole source of the social security of individuals
in Thailand. This means that 'relationships', in the Western
one-to-one sense, must be subordinated to the need to sus-
tain parents, grandparents, children and siblings. Sometimes
the survival of a whole network of people depends upon their
earnings. When Western men discover this, they rarely
understand its significance and see it instead as a personal
betrayal, an affront to their generosity and good faith.

A book like this one inevitably raises more questions than
it can answer. What kind of people come to Thailand in
search of satisfactions that elude them at home? Do they
have a history of failed relationships, broken marriages, emotional disappointment, sexual discontent? Do they feel they
can make a fresh start in a strange society, where they cannot even speak the language? Do they imagine they can
remain unknown in a social context unfamiliar to them? Are
they looking for a place to hide? What keeps so many of
them coming back, even when they speak – as many do – in
negative terms of their experience here?

For me, one of the most interesting elements emerging
from these pages is the way in which we rationalise our
behaviour when it is at its most irrational – in the pursuit of
the tangle of love, affection and sex; and that this often
conceals a licence for sexist and racist behaviour which
would no longer be tolerated in the West. In many ways, the
sex tourist embodies archaic and disgraced social values, and
can give vent to forms of power which would not pass unchallenged at home.

Much has been written about the sex industry in Thailand and the focus has been primarily on the women, their
struggles, the exploitation and abuse they must suffer, their
often heroic efforts to survive; all of these are, I hope, also

reflected here. But the purpose of this work is also to reach some more difficult questions about the purposes and direction of forms of development that have caught up the destinies of rich Westerners with those of poor country migrant women and men in Thailand. What has set whole populations in movement in this way, what kind of uprootings and dislocations link the livelihood of the daughters of rice farmers with the vacation or retirement trip, the gilded migrations of Western tourists? And what are the consequences for some of the receiving countries? This is why the book is also concerned with the growing traffic in young women and children, as well as with the spread of HIV and AIDS. It is intended to be both a guide and help to those involved in human rights campaigns and a support to movements which are trying to modify some of the more damaging consequences of what is recorded here.

2

THE ENVIRONMENT OF
THE SEX TRADE

I

Bangkok is one of the most badly congested and polluted
cities in Asia. Its population more than doubled from 2.4
million people in 1965 to 5 million in 1985, and has
probably doubled again within the last decade. The precise
figures are unknown, because at any given time, the population is swollen by up to 2 million seasonal migrant
workers, whose identity card was issued elsewhere and who
do not count as residents of Bangkok. Many migrants live
in barracks on construction sites, in shared rooms in hot
airless tenements, in slums overhanging the polluted *klongs*
(canals). Officially, 17 per cent of the people live in slums;
a figure considered by many non-governmental organisations to be an underestimate.

There have been large-scale clearances of urban poor settle-
ments as Bangkok has taken on the aspect of a highly developed Western city, its skyline dominated by huge office blocks,
financial and corporate headquarters, shopping malls, condominiums and hotels for the 6 million tourists who now visit
annually.

The state of the urban environment of Bangkok is well
known; not only in terms of the air quality, pollution, labour
conditions, but also in the sheer amount of time it takes
people to get to work – journeys of two or three hours each
way are commonplace. This contrast, between the modern
and efficient façade of the city and the quality of life within

it is just one example of a preoccupation with appearances and the importance of a cultural concern with 'saving face.'

The commitment of Thais to the avoidance of conflict does make Bangkok a safe city: you can walk around anywhere, day or night, without threat or the fear that haunts London or New York. Social peace has been maintained in a country which has been the site of an epic upheaval and driven economic transformation in the past 20 years. It is perhaps the absorptive capacity of Thai people which helps to account for the relative calm here, their ability to tolerate what seem to outsiders unbearable degrees of exploitation (workers, many of them little more than children, virtual industrial captives in assembly and manufacturing units, especially in the suburbs), oppression and social injustice (the poorest 20 per cent earn a mere 4 per cent of the wealth).

Nowhere is the discrepancy between rhetoric and reality more clear than in official attitudes to the sex trade and sex tourism. Prostitution is illegal, under the Prostitution Suppression Act of 1960. Yet the Entertainment Places Act barely six years later, in 1966, regulated nightclubs, dance halls, bars, massage parlours, baths and places 'which have women to attend male customers'. Soon after this Act was passed, Thailand came to an agreement with the US military to allow US soldiers stationed in Vietnam to use Thailand for rest and recreation. By 1970, spending in Thailand by US military personnel exceeded 20 million dollars.

Early in January 1996, the government of Banharn Silpa-Archa gave an order that all bars and clubs should close by 1 a.m. rather than at the then prevailing time of 2 a.m. This was duly hailed as a 'crackdown' on the sex trade and widely reported in the Western media. For a few days, many places of entertainment did indeed close their doors somewhat earlier; but within a few weeks, it was back to 'normal', that is, at three in the morning, the streets around Patpong were thronged with tourists, bars were just closing and the hotels used by the sex industry were still humming.

In the gap between the official version and the lived experience, much of the life of Bangkok in particular, and Thailand in general, is defined. To provide some insight into the circumstances in which each year millions of male tourists now seek sexual adventure in a country where prostitution is banned, I monitored the English language press for evidence of the social, moral and political climate in which this paradox can flourish. The pretence may seem hypocritical to foreigners. Perhaps it is this perception which makes them think they can get away with doing things here which they cannot do at home: they believe the culture of institutionalised mendacity gives them licence to do as they please. This apparent freedom has to be understood for what it is. There is indeed a space afforded by corruption on the one hand and also by a certain permissiveness on the part of authority, as long as that authority is not challenged. One Thai friend, a university lecturer, expressed it like this: 'As long as the people of Thailand let the government get on with its real business, which is making money, then the people will be left alone to do more or less as they like. But let them not call into question the activities of government or they will find just how limited their freedoms are.'

'Saving face' as a traditional means of avoiding conflict, is sometimes seen as one of those 'Asian values' which are so much admired now by certain Western politicians. But saving face is increasingly for foreign consumption: to present a pleasing appearance to outsiders of the Asian 'tiger' economies: Thailand's economic growth has been around 8 or 9 per cent for many years. Investors, bankers, creditors, dignitaries from abroad, who come here in great numbers, must be preserved at all costs from exposure to some of the asperities of a society which has seen growing social injustice as a consequence of its growth and 'development'.

II

On 1 and 2 March 1996, the Asia-Europe meeting in Bangkok was attended by the heads of government of most European countries, as well as those of Southeast Asia. The government declared two days of public holiday, so that the visitors should be spared any contact with the true horrors of Bangkok's traffic and pollution.

At the time of the Asia-Europe meeting, a group of farmers were marching from the Prime Minister's own constituency towards Bangkok to protest at the usurpation of their ancestral lands for the construction of a local government administration complex. The contractor for this work of indispensable development happened to be a close friend of the Prime Minister. Fearing the arrival of disaffected country people in the capital at the time of the international meeting, a group of government ministers went by helicopter to dissuade them from turning up while important foreigners were in town. The protesters complied.

At about the same time, it was revealed that parts of Bangkok have a dust-particle level of 3000 mg per cubic foot, over ten times the safe limit. In response, the Bangkok Municipal Authority announced that teams of street cleaners would sweep the dust away. Conspicuously, yellow dustcarts appeared, parked close to where squads of blue-uniformed workers assembled on the sidewalk, mainly it seems, for the benefit of the public, while they received instruction in the seriousness of their task. The dust level, exacerbated ironically by the construction of the slowest fast-transit transport system in the world, was not expected to diminish.

The government announced changes in banking hours: instead of opening between 8.30 a.m. until 3 p.m., banks would now open from 10 a.m. to 4 p.m. This measure, the government solemnly informed people, would reduce traffic by 40 per cent. There was no detectable change.

It was revealed that the increase in suicides in Thailand between 1994 and 1995 was more than 60 per cent. That means more than 22,000 people, or 45 per 100,000, took their own lives. Social discontinuity, migration, the breaking of families, extreme competitiveness, are offered as causes. A young woman suffering from AIDS, abandoned by family and friends, leaps to her death from a hospital window. A 17-year-old student, unable to discuss with his parents the pressures upon him to achieve in the school examination system, kills himself. I met a young man who committed suicide while I was in Bangkok (see pages 69–70).

During September and October 1995, there was severe flooding in the city. Deforestation, environmental degradation in the north of the country prevented the heavy monsoon rains from being absorbed by the earth and the water ran off all at once. Swollen streams and rivers flowed into the Chao Phraya River, which, when it reached Bangkok, eventually rose to 2.27 metres above sea level, the highest for a century.

Low-lying areas of the city were frequently under water, especially Thonburi and the eastern suburbs. In places the water was very deep; some bridges over the river had to be closed. As time went by, roads on the western side of the river were also affected: the water fell and rose with the ebb and flow of the tides. People sandbagged their shops and houses. In one restaurant the workers were cooking, knee-deep in water; the men were plucking the last feathers from the throat and breast of geese and turning the golden carcasses on a spit over a scarlet fire. In the factories open to the street, ice crushers were working in water; the beaters of gold leaf hammered with wooden mallets, seated in water, the cleaners of engine parts were performing their labour stooped permanently in water. Some houses became part of the river and as the boats passed, they sent rising waves into the already flooded interiors; duckweed and water lilies floated through front doors, together with dead fish, rotting animal carcasses, snakes and foul odours. The electricity supply was interrupted; cars were abandoned in flooded streets. People walked barefoot, sometimes holding aloft fashionable new shoes, even though when they stepped from the water, their feet were gashed by jagged metal or glass.

The government had been issuing reassurances for the past two months. The floods would not get worse, the river defences were being strengthened, pumps would remove any floodwater. Some places in Thonburi had been flooded since 20 August. On 28 October, the high tide was higher than the peak in 1942 and more than 20 square kilometres of the city were under water. In Tan Nawa, 90 centimetres of water spread into one area, because people living on the other side of the road had been living in stagnant water and they had removed the sandbags which permitted the water to reach areas hitherto dry. The government blamed the people for the flooding. Ratchadamnoen Nai Avenue in front of the Grand Palace became a canal when Sunam Luang was flooded. City officials were still reassuring the people of Bangkok even as the embankments burst. The Prime Minister promised new permanent flood walls along both sides of Chao Phraya River. He ordered city officials to build wooden walkways so that flood victims could make their way to get drinking water and food.

Nothing happened. The flood was a metaphor. The shadow-play of governance lapses as soon as the crisis is past. Authority only has to speak and it is as though it were done; anyone who denies it is unpatriotic. Similarly, anyone who says that Thailand is the centre of an international sex industry is defaming the country, ruining its image abroad.

The Don Muang Tollway Company is making a loss on its fast motorway to the airport: it is blaming the government which had promised to demolish two flyovers which would have forced motorists to use the tollway.

There is a meeting for the press of non-governmental organisations just before the Asia-Europe meeting. Of the 200 people present at this meeting, at least 40 are from police and security agencies. They are easily recognisable – they register as journalists representing newspapers and magazines that have long ceased to exist.

It is revealed that in some parts of the country, more than 90 per cent of farmers are suffering from pesticide poisoning. A 1993 survey showed that of 3434 northern farmers, 3299 suffered pesticide poisoning; 44 died in 1993. In 1994, 3143 were poisoned and 41 died. Blood tests on over 400,000 farmers in 1995 found high concentrates of cholinesterase, an enzyme found in pesticides, in 78,481 of them.

In 1989, the government introduced a financial package to assist farmers who had suffered as a result of typhoon Gay. This offered loans at 5 per cent interest. Politicians and local well-to-do farmers exploited loopholes by having poor farmers acquire loans on their behalf. 'Influential persons', in collaboration with officials of the Bank of Ayutthaya and Agricultural Co-Operatives, had taken several hundred million baht (25 baht = 1 US dollar), a figure, said the Deputy Finance Minister, 'not as high as the one billion baht as reported in the press'. He said he would instruct the bank to be more strict in extending loans to farmers.

The air at Saphan Kwai, the poorest in the city, will worsen in 1996, according to a senior environmental official, because of the construction of a station on the elevated train project in an already over-developed area. This would trap more dust and pollutants. Researchers from Mahidol University identified 13 pathogenic fungi species and 16 pathogenic bacteria species in the city's dust. One million people in

Bangkok suffer from dust-induced allergies. The concrete pillars of the elevated railway darken the sky and create a permanent gloom, especially in the rain.

Land Reform officials surrendered to the Crime Suppression Division, after being accused of involvement in a scandal over the redistribution of land to poor farmers under the Chuan Leek Pai government. Fifteen wealthy people in Phuket had benefited from the distribution of land deeds which were revoked last year. Ineligible recipients included the husband of an MP and her father-in-law.

Farmers in Roi-et calling for eucalyptus trees to be cut down threaten to shift their week-long rally to Government House in Bangkok, if their demands are not met. Two thousand farmers from eight northeastern provinces camping outside Roi-et City Hall for a week want the eucalyptus trees replaced by fruit trees. They claim – correctly – that eucalyptus robs the soil of moisture and degrades the quality of soil, so that nothing grows and wildlife is destroyed.

About 0.28 per cent of donated blood distributed to hospitals throughout the country is HIV-infected; that is, 2000 units out of 700,000. In the six months from September 1995 to February 1996, 38 patients were infected with HIV through donated blood.

A series of fires in shopping malls and cinemas in Bangkok have reduced cinema attendances. Cinema bosses say they are tightening safety in shopping malls. The director of the Entertain Golden Village Company, which has 16,800 seats in 62 theatres, says measures taken include 'fire-resistant walls that can hold a blaze at bay for two hours, 80 per cent wool carpets which produce non-toxic fumes and smoke and heat detectors'. In seven fires in recent months, police investigations proved inconclusive. Arson to collect insurance is suspected but cannot be proved. In any case, the malls are high-profit, low-cost structures, the building is skimped, sprinklers do not work, fire regulations are rarely observed.

A radio programme called *Different Perspectives* is taken off the air. It is too controversial and critical of government. The company, Media Plus, had leased the frequency from the military. It is told by senior government officials to terminate the programme, for fear of political repercussions. The programme had interviewed the Prime Minister in a way that he was said to have found humiliating, since he had no answers to the questions posed. A government spokesman said, 'You have not seen us order the closure of any newspaper or any political discussion show on radio, even though these have been highly critical of the government.'

The Bangkok Bank of Commerce is on the brink of insolvency, because of sweetheart loans made by bank officials to a group of government MPs. It costs two billion baht of taxpayers' money to save the bank.

The Army Commander-in-Chief, Pramon Palasin, renewed his call for army officers who provide protection or debt collection services to turn over a new leaf. Some army personnel have been collecting considerable sums of money, working as bouncers for entertainment venues or debt collectors.

The employers' organisation of Thailand says that the annual increase in the minimum wage should be scrapped, because it deters investors and fuels inflation. The increase demanded by employees from 145 to 200 baht (from 6 to 8 US dollars) a day is 'excessive'. Viroj Amattakulchai, of the Thai Garment Industry Employers, says the minimum wage of Thailand has now surpassed that of Vietnam, China and Indonesia.

The investigation into the Tha Chana illegal logging scandal concludes. Eight people, including the former Deputy Agricultural Minister and the Director-General of the Forestry Department were implicated. Concessions were granted to companies in 1987 to grow rubber trees in parts of the Tha Chana national forest reserve. An inquiry exonerates the politicians and blames a former Forestry Department Director-General for failing to implement the 1993 order of Deputy Agricultural Minister to terminate concessions that caused a conflict of local interests.

The former Labour Department Director admits that economic growth has widened inequalities which has created a 'social crisis'. The average industrial wage is now 5000 baht a month (200 US dollars) for a 60-hour week. The GDP increase per capita over 30 years has been 30 per cent, but real wages have risen by 3 per cent. Thirty years ago, 1.7 million children were working, mainly in agriculture. There are now 5 million children working, half of them in manufacturing, the rest in the commercial and service sector, including the sex and entertainment industries. In 1960, there were 6 million working women; this had risen to 12 million by 1995, with up to 5 million in the sex and entertainment industries. There are an estimated 200,000 prostitutes in the country. There are now half a million drug addicts and more than half a million who are HIV positive.

A government committee opts to let the Expressway and Rapid Transit Authority take over the troubled Don Muang Tollway Company. The tollway cost 13 billion baht and has debts of 7 billion.

A court in the USA will decide whether to release on bail a former MP charged with smuggling 49 tons of marijuana into the US.

A plan by the Deputy Prime Minister, Chavalit Yongchaiyudh, to set up a bank for needy war veterans would benefit investors, claims a Democrat MP, since this is the real intention of the scheme. Applicants seeking licences include a real estate company which is a shareholder in the Thai Danu Bank, a group with shares in the Thai Farmers' Bank, a group with shares in Asia Bank and two media owners.

Fire razed a noodle factory: the Kaka Instant Noodle factory was destroyed by sparks from a welding machine that was installing an air conditioning unit. Damage reached 50 million baht (2 million US dollars). The welding employee was arrested and charged with negligence.

There is disagreement between non-governmental organisations and the government on the new Community Forest Laws. Drafting the laws is supposed to have been a compromise between villagers and their representatives and government. Government officials insist that government retains the power to relocate villages from 'environmentally sensitive forest areas', while the NGOs say that villagers have managed the forests sustainably for centuries. The 'compromise' appears to the NGOs to leave government free to offer contracts to their supporters and dependants to continue to plunder the depleted forests, while those who live in them will be further marginalised.

The Thai-Burma border should be re-opened at Mae Hong Son, according to the provincial Chamber of Commerce: officials have been taking advantage of the closed border to take bribes to allow Burmese and Thai traders to transport cattle or logs. They were also accused of charging 3500 baht per car and 500 for each motorcyclist to pass through the checkpoint.

A time bomb is discovered under the car of an industrialist, who suspects his ex-wife because he believes she fears he will not share his wealth with their children.

The legality of the issuance of upgrading ownership documents into land rights to the Tancharoen family is to be investigated by the House Local Administration Committee. It was alleged that Deputy Interior Minister Suchart Tancharoen had abused his power to issue ownership papers to his own family.

Hundreds of villagers demanding more compensation for land they will have to leave for the Hong Ngu Hao airport in Samut Prakan (the province that adjoins Bangkok), called off their rally after the government ignored their demands for 1 million baht per 50 square *wah* (200 square metres). The Deputy Agriculture Secretary told them the compensation package was already agreed – each family will get 800,000 baht, or 50 square *wah* elsewhere with a relocation fee of 50,000 baht. One thousand families are affected. The airport project will cost 10 billion baht.

Thailand has become the 'battlefield' for rival European defence manufacturers and contractors seeking to supply the Armed Forces with modern weapons systems under the 100 billion baht defence budget. Thirty-two foreign arms manufacturers have agents and contractors stationed in Bangkok.

The University Council of Ramkhamhaeng declares that the thesis of the Prime Minister is original and will not pay heed to allegations that it is plagiarised. The President of the Council said, 'The university would be viewed as having an uncertain stance if it decided to investigate the allegation that the thesis was copied. The University Council will not compare the thesis with another research paper. Those who want to make the comparison can do so at the university library.' It was alleged that the thesis was copied from a research paper prepared for the Interior Ministry by the Prime Minister's supervisor; this man is now a minister in the Prime Minister's Office.

A doll factory is damaged by fire and 200 million baht worth of damage occurs. Three hundred workers had just gone off shift. The incident recalls the fire at the Kader Doll factory in 1993 where 188 workers were killed.

Street vendors are cleared from around the hotels where delegates to the Asia-Europe meeting will stay. They will be deprived of their livelihood for two days. One hundred and fifty million baht are spent on hiring or borrowing 165 Mercedes-Benz cars for the delegates; a 200 million baht facelift is announced for the Queen Sirikit Convention Centre where the meeting will take place.

Scientists say that a strain of HIV prevalent in Thailand spreads more easily among heterosexuals than the US strain. This 'could pose a threat if it takes hold in the US'.

The son of the Chart Thai Party deputy leader, Mr Poonphol Asavahame, faced a charge of attempted murder, when he allegedly shot a man after a car accident. He was freed on a bail of 20,000 baht. Originally he was charged only with assault: a building contractor accidentally bumped his pickup truck into the rear of the brand new Jaguar sedan. The contractor was beaten up and fired at and a shot grazed his head. Fearing injustice from the police, he and his stepdaughter sought help from Democratic Party activists. Mr Poonphol was treated like a VIP at the police station.

Animal feed containing growth-stimulating chemicals must be reclassified from being a food to being a drug. The warning comes amid fears that people who eat meat products also ingest the chemicals and, over time, become immune to antibiotics. The new ruling applies to many poultry farmers. Deputy Secretary of the Food and Drug Administration, General Narong Kunaphiban, says that manufacturers of animal feed containing chemicals like chlortetracycloine, oxytetracycline, lincomycin and spiramycin must register their products as medicines or face up to three years in prison and a 5000 baht fine.

Human rights are not on the agenda of the Asia-Europe meeting. 'Some Southeast Asian nations are not ready to talk about it', says the Prime Minister. As host and chairman, he does not want to see issues raised which could lead to vast differences of opinion between participants during the discussions at the summit.

Here are some of the elements that go to create the invisibility of a conspicuous sex industry: economic and social laissez-faire; a disdain by the rulers of Thailand for the unprivileged; an avoidance of conflict entirely on the terms of the most advantaged; a deeply rooted view of the poor which sees them as a lesser order of human being, a caste-based indifference whereby the fate of the poor is of no consequence. Just how far these views are of a piece with the attitudes of many Western visitors to Thailand will emerge in the following pages.

3

MALE VISITORS TO BANGKOK: FOREIGN RESIDENTS, VISITORS AND TOURISTS

I

Ken retired in 1992 from the Milk Marketing Board in Britain. His job was to drive trucks around the farms of Northern England, collecting the milk and taking it to the central depot for distribution. Before that, he drove petrol tankers for 20 years; a job he quit because of boredom: 'With petrol, you don't even load the tanker, you just drive it from the docks to its destination, somebody else does everything. At least with the milk, you got to meet people. I could see that the Milk Marketing Board was being wound up, so I left.'

Ken is a heavy man, with silver-grey hair, a gentle face and pleasant manner. His has been a conspicuously successful relationship with a Thai; although, he says, it is far from typical.

I came to Thailand for the first time after my divorce. We'd been married 17½ years. I had a girl 15, a boy 13. It was my son who told me that my wife was cheating on me. He had tears in his eyes when he told me. I didn't know anything about it.

In spite of that, she got custody of the children. It ended up in bitterness and a lot of hurt. After that, I swore I would never go with another woman. But I was persuaded to come on holiday to Thailand with a mate of mine. We went to Pattaya. I picked up a girl who stayed with me for the fortnight we were there. She was very good to me. She helped me overcome the pain of parting from my wife.

I went with her one day speed-skiing on the sea. She turned round suddenly to say something to me, and the boat overturned. We both went into the water. She panicked and went under. I dived down and brought her up. I felt fine. But the next day I turned blue; I'd taken in so much water. As a result I have a permanent lung problem. In fact, I'm just going back home to England because I have a hospital appointment. I only have half of my right lung.

She sat by my bedside day and night for three days. I mean, I'd only just met her, I was nothing to her, she didn't have to stay. She went to get the medicine the doctor prescribed, paid for it out of her own money. That was my introduction to Thai women, so you might say I was prejudiced in favour of them.

Then after I was feeling better, I sent her home in the evening; I thought it was probably best if she got home before it was too late, and I wanted to put her in a taxi. I didn't speak Thai, so I asked this woman who was passing by to help me. She put the girl in a taxi, made sure she was safe. I looked at her, and something clicked. I said, 'Would you like to go for a meal, no strings.' She agreed.

We sat for five hours in the restaurant. I learned more about her in five hours than I had found out about my wife in 17 years of marriage. And it went from there. She became my wife.

Her father had pissed off when she was four. She had one brother who was blind. He was a musician and was married. She had been farmed out to an aunt as a child, because her mother couldn't keep her after the husband went away. Auntie turned out to be a millionaire, or at least, very rich. She has a lot of land; but she controlled everybody around her with a rod of iron, including Loy, my wife. We have now bought some land in Sonburi, about 120 miles from Bangkok. I send Loy's mother 5000 baht a month, which she is well pleased with; she has never been so well off in her life.

I'm very happy. They are good people. Loy can't do enough for me; as a matter of fact, it gets too much sometimes, but if I say anything, she is hurt. She does things for me which I can actually do quite well for myself; in fact, in all my years of the first marriage, it would never have occurred to my wife to do it. Yet this woman is very intelligent. She has two degrees. When I met her, she was working in a hotel in Bangkok. Within two weeks of landing in

Britain, she had got a job in a hotel there; just an ordinary job. She doesn't want responsibility at work. She sees looking after me as a full-time job. Yet she's been offered a position in management, she is very capable. I say to her, being realistic, 'If anything happens to me, what will you do?' She doesn't want to hear it, but that's life. I'm optimistic, I've only got half a lung. I'm going to see a specialist, anything could happen. But in Bangkok I can't breathe, I can't stand the pollution, I feel suffocated in the city.

We live in Preston. There is quite a big Thai community in Lancashire, Blackburn, Blackpool, Preston. In fact, I have a solicitor friend whom I advise on some of the cases that come up, Thai girls who've married Brits mainly. There is one Thai girl, she had been married for four years and her husband wanted to get rid of her. He put all his assets, the business, the house and the money in his own name, so she would have no claim on it. We managed to get that changed, so she got her share of everything when they split up. The Thais get shat on by the British. I don't like to say it, but it's generally true.

Of course, you can't get them into the country now. It took me six months, even in 1988. The stories I've heard about what happens to Thais: a lot of them have no one to turn to, in a foreign, often hostile country. If they lose their relationship they are really on their own. It's unnatural, the way we live. I've never experienced such sweetness and affection. I now realise I'd never known what love is; and I thought I did, having been married 17 years.

When she came into the UK, she had a medical examination, just to be sure. She was 30 then; now she's 36. I only came to Bangkok last week to take her home to her mother. If I hadn't insisted, she would never have come without me. She didn't want to leave me. This is actually the first day in six years we have been apart. She'll be coming in another nine days anyway; but I wanted her to see her family.

I don't know what will happen. I'm not a pessimist, but she is 25 years younger than me; she'll have to make a life for herself eventually. But Loy is the best thing that ever happened to me. I miss my children, of course; but I've found something that has made life a thousand times better than I'd ever dreamed it could be. And it took going to Thailand to find it.

When I met Greg, a New Zealander of about 40, he was sitting in Lumpini Park, looking, as he said, for the second most rare thing in Bangkok: fresh air. And what's the rarest? Love. According to Greg, the commonest thing in Bangkok is sex. Greg is a builder from Auckland, self-employed, married but separated from his wife. He has one child who lives with his wife. He has built himself a new house, but he complains,

It's empty. What's the point of having a beautiful place if there's no one to enjoy it? I can't stand being there on my own. I'm a workaholic. The worst thing that can happen to me is leisure; weekends, public holidays. I try to organise my life so I'm working even when everybody else is having a good time.

I want to find somebody to share my life. Maybe I'm picky, but I can't find anyone at home. I've been through some women, I can't remember the names of half of them. That's what brought me here. I came with a friend at first, but I don't know, I felt embarrassed, going off and doing everything in pairs. I've come on my own this time. I'm looking. But I don't think this is the right place either.

In Thailand, money is the biggest aphrodisiac. I mean it. It is the most gigantic turn on for women. It's no good saying to them 'I can't afford it, I don't have it'; they do not believe you. Because they could never imagine going to New Zealand or Australia, they assume that anybody who can afford to come to Thailand must be loaded. And compared to them, I suppose we are. They ask how much it costs to fly; and when you say it, you can see them thinking 'Oh he must be rich.'

I've often thought about it in the bars. Some of the blokes there are repulsive, old, fat, ugly. Yet these women gaze into their eyes, pat their pot belly, caress their baldness, as though this is what they really want. I mean, I love Thai women. I think they're sensual, very skilled, very attractive. They know how to make love by instinct. But I don't believe in them. I want to know what they would make of me if I had nothing. I've tried giving them just a small tip, a couple of hundred, to see if they respond according to the amount you give. I think they do. If you give 1500 or 1000, you get a fairly ecstatic response; if you give 500, it's a bit lukewarm. A couple of hundred, it's definitely polite rather than enthusiastic. Before you take them off (that is, pay the bar to take them out) they'll treat everybody as though they're God's gift; but then next time, there's definitely a cooling off.

But you ask yourself, how far does she like me, which is what she shows, and how far does she like my money? And there is no answer to it. Without money, you don't go to Bangkok, so the question doesn't arise. You can't separate the two. So it's money that makes every guy who walks into a bar desirable. That's why they don't mind the beer gut or the baldness – they just see the wallet, which is the sexiest organ on a man's body.

I've thought about it a lot. I've been here seven or eight times now. I like it, I have a good time. But after, it makes being alone much worse. I wouldn't want to get involved with the women I've met, even though I'm always on the lookout for the one who's different. The thing is, it is a particular skill, that's why they're in the bars – they can do the necessary play-acting, they can convince the punter that he's what they've been waiting for all their life. And because you are at the centre of your own life, you don't think 'Oh she'll be doing the same thing with somebody else tomorrow or next week.' You think you're special or different. You're not. The question most farangs don't ask is, 'Why do these particular women go into the sex trade and not into working in a department store?' The women who go into factories, a lot of them are just as attractive; maybe they don't have the ability to play the part with conviction. The bars, it's theatre, it's show business. They're good actresses, that's one of the qualifications for the job.

But I don't think it matters. It only becomes a problem if you want to be loved for yourself and not for your money. The two can't be separated. And that's because it's not about love, but about survival. She's got to eat, her family have got to live; and you make that possible. But don't start getting romantic about them, or you're a lost man. So why do I keep coming back? Hope is the answer. Hope against hope. Bangkok is a place where affairs are always starting. Even when they end, you're looking around for the next adventure.

Harry is in his fifties. I met him in a hotel restaurant at lunchtime. The tables are covered with greasy plastic cloths, a small vase of dingy grey and yellow mottled orchids (real). A television plays noisily above the bar. The waiters watch TV abstractedly while serving the customers. Harry has worked his way almost to the end of one bottle of Sing Thip Thai whisky; the ice in the metal pail has melted and the outside is frosted with condensation. I am sitting at a neighbouring table. Harry beckons to me to join him. It is clear he wants to talk. 'Don't believe anything you hear about Thailand. The women, they're arseholes. I should know, I married one.'

Harry emigrated with his family from England to Australia when he was a child, just after the Second World War. He began his working life in a bank and in his early twenties he was posted to Papua New Guinea. There, he saw opportunities for business, so he left the bank and started up his own shop, a dry-goods store, in Port Moresby.

Fifteen years ago, I had everything going for me. I was making money, I had a charmed life, I was a millionaire. Then I met Daeng. She walked into my store one day and asked for a job. I made a terrible mistake. Instead of putting her behind the counter, I put her in my bed. And I have lived to regret it.

The only thing I don't regret is our son. Sammy. A beautiful kid. I'd give anything to have him with me, to take him out doing the kind of thing any father expects to do with his boy – fishing, golfing, climbing and swimming. But I can't. I can't get him out of Thailand. And I can't get him out of the clutches of that bitch.

What I didn't know the day she walked into my life was that she had been taken to Papua New Guinea by another guy, who had found out what a shit she was and left her there, destitute. She knew where to come to find another sucker.

You don't realise in the beginning. In fact, as long as we had money, everything was fine. She sure could spend it. She was the best dresser in Moresby; and she still looks good. She's now back in her home town, Lampang, in the North.

It was nearly time for me to retire. By 1992, I'd had

enough; so I sent her back to Lampang with the money to buy a house there. It cost 1.2 million baht, that's about 50,000 US dollars. I bought it in her name. I was kind of commuting from Papua New Guinea to Thailand, but I thought when I'd wound up the business there, I'd be coming here to settle down and spend my life just being a father and husband, enjoying it. She wanted to open a business in Lampang, but I said, 'No, the time for that is over.' We have a house, an income of about 5000 US dollars a month – that is a high income in Thailand, although less than we'd had before. I said, 'We'll just have to live more modestly.' Modest living and Daeng didn't exactly go together.

What I didn't know was that she had mortgaged the house while I was still in Papua New Guinea. Not only that, she'd done the same with the Toyota sedan that I'd bought her. When I got to Lampang, she asked me for more money. I hit the roof. 'I'm not paying for the house twice over, or the bloody car.' I'd given her money to pay the bills and none of them had been paid. She wanted money and more money.

All this time, while I stayed back in Papua New Guinea, she was screwing around. Now she's got a Police Captain in tow. You can never get the better of these people. They'll stick together, they'll conspire, make a plan to bleed you of every penny you've got.

Harry drains the bottle of Sing Thip and pours water from the ice pail into it. The waiter comes and asks him if he wants another. 'Just one more.' He means another bottle.

Trouble is, I have a drink problem. Always have had. My first wife had a lot to put up with from me. She was Australian Chinese, a lovely woman. We're better friends now than we ever were while we were married. She lives in Brisbane. I can't blame her for leaving me. I'm an alcoholic. At least I know it.

I left Lampang this time because they tried to kill me. Three policemen came to the house with her Captain, carrying rocks. I got hit on the head twice and once in the eye. I crawled out of the house for help and what did she do? She jumped in the car and tried to run over me. I can't do a thing about it, because he is a police officer. I left town, because I wanted to get away with my life.

'But I love my son, I'd do anything for him. I thought maybe I could take him out of the country, through the Malaysian border. Trouble is, I have a Papua New Guinea passport. It seemed like a good idea at the time, it sort of showed the government that I was committed to the country; it helped with business, it saved all the bureaucratic hassles over visas and all that. It doesn't look very sensible from where I am now.

I stay in this hotel because it's a gay hotel and they leave me alone. They know I'm not interested and there's no women around to give me the come-on. I can drink, nobody interferes with me. The other guys round here, most of them are looking for boys, they've got their own problems. I don't mind that, as long as they leave me be. But sometimes, you need to talk to a farang and they've got no time for you, because they're always on the lookout for whatever their particular obsession is.

In Lampang, there's a lignite mine, a Thai-Australian joint venture and quite a few Australians are working and living there. Nearly all of them can tell a similar story. They were taken for a ride by women they picked up for a one-nighter and who took them to the cleaners over a year, two years, five years. One guy in Lampang bought a house, 1.5 million baht. He came home one day and was met by his wife's sister. She just said to him, 'You don't live here any more.' And that was it. He didn't. There wasn't a thing he could do about it.

They're a treacherous lot. Don't believe a word they tell you and you may survive, but I wouldn't bank on it. They're good at acting. Don't get involved. They're arseholes. A farang can never win, they'll stick together and they'll make a plan to relieve him of every penny he's got.

Harry goes up to his room and returns with the photograph album he carries everywhere. It is crammed with pictures of his son, now seven; on holiday, holding a balloon, at Christmas with a new toy, in England: a picture taken on the South Downs, above Hove, where Harry's mother lived. She returned to England when her husband died in his fifties.

She died in 1994. Harry says of his son,

I should have kept him there, in England. I was tempted. But I can't take him away from his mother, even if she is a bitch. Maybe she loves him. My first wife couldn't have children, so when he came along I was already getting on and it was such a thrill. I thought my whole life would change. I mean, I knew she was screwing around even then. I knew, but somehow I didn't want to know. You can put these things out of your mind and it's not until people start telling you what is going on under your nose and they give you the proof, that your eyes are opened.

Anyway, even if I took him to Australia, England, what could I do for him? I've got to get off this first. If you do it drastically, in 48 hours, the shock can kill you. You should reduce gradually, over a matter of months. This is what I'm trying to do. I used to drink a bottle of Scotch in the morning.

I've known the Prime Minister of Papua New Guinea for years, Julius Chan. He once told me, if I come off the piss, he'll make me Consul for Papua New Guinea in Bangkok. That would give me some power over the bastards. That's why I left Lampang. I felt scared for my life. This is serious stuff.

He caresses the portrait of the child with a tender, unsteady hand; his eyes fill with tears. He takes another sip of Thai whisky.

I do know one Australian who married a Thai and is happy. She was a hooker; now she's in her fifties. They met in Patpong. They're happy. At the time, you wouldn't have rated their chances, but that's it. You can't say what will work, you can't say what will be a disaster. That's life I guess. At least, that's my life. I've done everything. I've caught 50-pound Papua New Guinea sea bass, I've bred Dobermans, I've had my own business, I've been rich. All over now. I don't know what I'll do. I haven't spoken to a farang for two weeks. First thing, I've got to come off this stuff. In Papua New Guinea, I was drinking two bottles of whisky a day. I'm not proud of that. Drinking this stuff, it's like kerosene. In the meantime, I've been here three weeks, 600 baht a day, wondering what the hell I'm going to do next.

II

Ray is British, in his late thirties, but he looks older. Deep ridges at the side of his mouth, pale blue eyes, long fair hair thinning. Tattoos on his arms, his left one almost completely covered by dense blue and red designs of women, in a circular mesh pattern, so they look like sea creatures caught in nets. He wears a tight T-shirt with an Adidas logo, and a growing beer belly overhangs the top of his jeans. I met him in the Pussy Galore bar, early one evening where I had gone to shelter from the rain. It was just before the music started, while the girls were arriving for work. Some were making up their faces in front of the horsehoe-shaped podium on which they would later parade and dance. The lightning of the storm threw an instant of dazzling whiteness over the dull interior, anticipating the strobes that would later take over. Ray was alone, looking down into his drink. He appeared thoughtful, melancholy. He doesn't even wait for me to ask a question, but said,

I don't know what I'm doing here. Looking for something I don't think exists. I met Nok here in Patpong four years ago. I'd already been through two marriages. I thought I knew all there was to know about women, none of it very nice. Nok taught me how little I knew. She never asked for anything at first. Whatever I gave her, she was grateful, always threw her arms round me. She took good care of me. She liked to lather my face before I shaved in the morning. She had a beautiful touch. She couldn't do enough for me.

That's how it was the first few times I came here. She would come to the airport to meet me, we would go to the Malaysia Hotel; not a very upmarket place, but it was free and easy, and we had some good times. At least I did. I wonder now what she made of it all. Was she just doing what she was paid for? It didn't seem like it at the time.

I think it was the fourth time I came, she looked worried. I asked her what was the matter. She said 'Nothing'. Then it came out, that her mother was sick and needed an operation. I recognise now that this was a familiar story. At the time, I just thought it was a problem; naturally, I wanted to help. I've become cynical. There's always a sick parent, a house destroyed by floods, a young brother to be put through school, a debt owing on some mortgaged land.

At first I gave. I felt good. I thought at least I was helping one poor family. She told me they didn't know she was work-ing in a bar, they would be very shocked. They thought she was a receptionist in a hotel. She said she was doing sex work to help the family. The family. Jesus, I thought I'd turned my back on families. I'd walked out on two of them; I've left three kids, two in Sunderland, one in Bristol. The last thing I was looking for was to take on somebody else's.

When the demands grew, I tried to resist. Boy, the tears, the sulks. 'You don't care about me.' I tried to tell her I was a working man, this was my holiday. She could speak enough English, but she pretended not to understand. Just money. Mai mee ngern. *That is the first phrase every foreigner learns here. Not hello or goodbye or what is your name. No, money:* mai mee ngern. *(He says it as though it were the name of a German city: Maimingen.)*

The point is, they know when they have you hooked, and they will play it to the last cent. That's why she asked for nothing in the beginning, pretended every little gift came as a surprise. They wait until they can do what they like with you. You think you're in control, because even though you might not be well off by Western standards, you still have more money than they do. They play you like a fruit machine. Sometimes you don't pay out, but if they carry on long enough, they'll hit the jackpot. These are very skilled ladies.

I was born in Newcastle. I've had money and I've spent it. I was a heavy goods driver, then a builder. I worked on constructing the big shopping centre in Gateshead. I believe in giving women a good time. That is my problem – I can give them a good time, but I can't stay married to them. I've lived with others, lasted maybe six months, a year, then you see some other piece of flesh that gives you the itch, and you've got to have it. My Mam and Dad never looked at anybody else. She died when she was still in her thirties. He made the house into a kind of shrine to her. It's still like that, pictures of her everywhere. After 25 years, he's never thought of anyone else. In a way, I envy him.

That's why I started coming here. I thought, 'Right, no strings. What you see is what you get, and what you get you pay for.' It all seemed very straightforward. But strings are not something you can see; it's only when they've been tied

*good and tight that you realise it isn't you who is in control,
it's them.*

*I was fucking obsessed with Nok. I woke up one day and
realised I couldn't go through the day without seeing her,
touching her. Fucking witchcraft. You know, they have all
this belief in ghosts and spirits – they're not wrong, it's us
who are wrong, taking life at face value. Face value is zero,
even if the face is bloody beautiful.*

*The more angry I got with her, the more quiet she became,
the less she said. She didn't cry, she just sat, rigid, no reaction.
I thought 'Yes, you dumb cow, I'll get a reaction out of you.' I
hit her. Not hard, but enough for her to feel it, to show her
who was boss. Which wasn't me, not by that time. It was a
stupid thing to do. A guy I knew hit a woman who fell and cut
her head; she went to hospital, and the police came and he
had to pay them 20,000 baht to get free.*

*But Nok didn't react. She just went and changed her
clothes. We had dinner. We went to bed. I said I was sorry.
We made love. It was one of the best nights I ever had. I
thought that was the end of it. It was. Next day, she went
out and didn't come back. I haven't seen her since. I went
round the bars looking for her. Gone. Somebody said she'd
gone to Chiang Mai. I went up there. No trace.*

*They drive you crazy. They do something to the man
inside you, and then they don't deliver. They're scheming,
cunning. They talk love, but the faraway look in their eyes is
because they're thinking dollars. A lot of guys say they like
Thai women, because Western women are too assertive.
Thai women get their way by appearing to give in, but
inside, they're hard as rock. I don't know which is worse.*

I asked Ray to talk about his experience of Western women
and why his marriages had failed. He said the difference
between Western women and Thai women is that Western
women taught him to hate and Thai women taught him to
cry. He didn't say this as though it were a tribute to them.

*I had a rough time with my first wife. She was shagging just
about every man who knocked at the door. I was driving at
that time, heavy goods vehicle. On some runs to Europe I'd
be away three or four days while she was partying at home.*

When I came home, you know how it is on the road, you're too tired to do anything, the road is still running past you in your sleep. She'd been waiting for me to come home, and I couldn't do anything. I can't blame her, but I was doing it for her and the kids, she didn't think of that. We were buying our own house, our parents had never been able to do that. I felt we were working together for some sort of improvement in our lives. I don't blame her now, but when I found out, I went crazy. I smashed up the house.

My second wife was just a panic reaction, because I thought a man can't live without a woman. She'd just left her husband, I'd known him when we were kids. He was a no-hoper, unemployed, unemployable. I took her in the cab with me across Europe a couple of times. Sex on wheels. Truckparks, a hotel, we'd do it anywhere. But she didn't want to stay at home at all. She got pregnant. I thought, 'This'll change her.' It didn't. Settling down was not what she had in mind. I called her Wanda Lust. She isn't a fit mother. And I'm not a fit father. So, pity the kids.

After that, I didn't have the heart to get married again. It seemed like a farce. By the time I came to Thailand, I was bitter. Then I got taken in all over again, because it was foreign, it was different. I felt strong. I felt I had nothing to lose, I wouldn't get involved. But then, when I'd been taken for another sucker, I just realised I'm not equal to them, women. What did you do in the sex war daddy? I lost.

I shan't make the same mistake again. You feel sorry for them, and you know they're poor. Because you have money, you feel strong; but the power money gives you is not strength. She took me up-country, Nakhon Ratchasima. Her house was one of the biggest in the village. She'd built it on the men who'd been through her; and by the size of that house, there'd been an awful lot of them. They make you feel like you are the first man in their life, even when you know they've been on the game for years.

It sounds like I hate women. I don't. The trouble is, maybe, I thought too much of them. I idolised my mother. She died when I was 15. I came home from school one day and she was dead on the floor. Just like that. There was an apple in her hand. She just sat there eating an apple, and she died. That was the biggest shock of my life. Nobody could live up to her.

This is what Bangkok does to you – it teaches you about yourself. Some lesson. I don't know if I'm a better person for it. I don't think so, because I don't trust anybody now. I come to Patpong, I look, I don't touch. Or if I do, I don't get involved. Never see her a second time. Even if you like them, you know it's all illusion.

That's how I feel at the moment anyway. I might change. But I'm not ready for another experience like those I've had. Maybe it's me. Maybe I just attract the kind of woman who'll walk all over me. I might look hard, but inside I'm soft. Most men are. I think women have an instinct. They know what they can get away with and what they can't.

Ray continually made as if to conclude the conversation, but then took off again; reluctant to stop talking, although he knew he was being reckless, indiscreet. As he spoke, his face became softer, his eyes shone with emotion. A man trapped; ashamed of an inner softness which he took for weakness. If this was how women saw him, it was because they were accepting his judgement of himself.

A number of meetings were like this; at bars, in hotel coffee-shops; people half-drunk. Bangkok is a city of unfulfilled desire; unfulfilled because it is a place where fantasies can be played out; and fantasies, acted out, are dangerous things. Bangkok also teaches that the dominators, too, need compassion; symapthy for the aggressors and the tormentors, because they are also in desperate want of emancipation, whether or not they recognise it.

X didn't tell me his name; all I discovered was that he was a Britisher living in Thailand, making one trip every six months to Malaysia or Singapore to get his visa renewed. In his fifties, thin, tough, fit. Especially fit; indeed, he prides himself he is among the fittest – those, he says, who survive. He loves parachuting, surfing, swimming, skiing (in Thailand?), and he travels around the country in his jeep, spending a few days here, a few days there. He rents a room for a few months in Bangkok in the rainy season, and then takes off again.

'I love Thailand', he says. 'The only problem is that it's full of Thais.' Then he added, in a parody of reaction to racist remarks, 'Some of my best friends are Thais.' He doesn't like the hassle or heat of Bangkok, but here, he says, people leave you alone to do whatever you want to do. Tolerance is a virtue he appreciates.

He doesn't like Britain, and doesn't 'believe in civilisation, Western or otherwise. All these people on the dole, all the scroungers in the UK, they should all be rounded up and brought to Bangkok, see how they'd survive. Better still, take them to Calcutta. Then they'd see what a thin veneer their civilisation is.' He came to Thailand 15 years ago because it was cheap. His income comes from rent on the house he owns, which is occupied by Social Security claimants – the very people he so despises.

But consistency is the last thing to look for in the exiles. Many are confused and unhappy. On the one hand, he says, 'I am what I have chosen to be'; and a few minutes later, 'This is my karma.' He says all the people he grew up with in Britain chose a marriage, a mortgage and a job. Now they are also finding out none of these things has given them any security. They are losing their jobs, their houses are being repossessed, their marriages are breaking up. He says this with detectable satisfaction. 'There is no security in life. No insurance, no money, no possessions: no other people can give that to you. What I like about Asia is that they recognise it; they don't give people illusions of security, where there is none.' I ask him if he thinks it a good idea for the limbless to wave their stumps at tourists to entreat their charity, or for women with children to be holding out a beaker every 20 metres along Charoenkrung. He shrugs, 'That's their fate; this is mine.' He wants to take credit for his own free choices, but he also wants to blame others for not doing the same thing.

He thinks Thailand would be better if it had been colonised. 'Look at what we gave to India. Railways, an administration, a system of government. If they chose to fuck it up after Independence, that's their business. But this country. Look at it. The corruption of the government stinks to heaven, if they say black is white, people believe it. Bangkok is chaos, and getting worse; nobody can sort it out. Look at the floods; the government says it will all be over in a few days, and half the city has been under water for three months. They worship the king and build a palace to burn the Princess Mother.' (He is referring to the fact that the mother of the king died in July 1995; the funeral structure was being prepared for her cremation in March 1996.) I say to him, 'If you like a free-for-all, I should think Thailand is exactly what you're looking for.' He says, 'Thailand, yes. Thais no. Talk about Buddhist culture, it's a heap of manure. They're about as Buddhist as I am, which is zilch. All this giggling and smiling, it gets on my nerves; it makes me want to smack them across the chops.'

I asked him why he stayed here. 'I told you, I came because it was cheap. It isn't now. I might have to move on. I can get what I want here.' Most of his interaction with Thai people is with women from the bars. 'I use them like I might use any other amenity, a restaurant or a public convenience. It answers my needs. No questions, no answers, no future. It's clean, it's efficient, it's over. I've never made the mistake of falling for them. Love in my book is a dirty word. Fuck isn't.' I wondered what would make him go back to England. For instance, would he return if he was sick or infirm? 'Not me. I'd take a pill that would send me into the big sleep. I don't want to lie on some hospital bed with tubes up my nose, wired up to a life-support system. I never think about the future. I live now. This is what I've chosen. Everybody is free to choose what they want. The only difference is most people start to whine about the consequences.' I protest that the sick and the weak do not choose to be as they are. And the rest of us, we may do what we choose, but what determines our choices? He has no time for such subtleties. 'Call me simple if you like', he replies, 'but that's my opinion. We had to have immigration controls in Britain, because all the scum of Asia would come flooding in if we didn't. When I come here, I'm not taking anybody else's job away. If they come there, they are. Then at the same time, they hold their hand out for anything that's going.'

In many of the wanderers through Asia, there is a strong vein of old imperialisms. It seems that my acquaintance was living in Thailand for the sense of superiority this confers on him. He didn't express it quite like that, but even his treatment of the waiters in the coffee shop suggested he didn't see them as equals. Because they were slow in serving him coffee, he went and helped himself from the glass coffee-jug on its stand over the flame. Several employees anxiously busied themselves around our table. 'See', he said, 'they can't cope if anybody does anything slightly out of the ordinary. They're conformist. That's why they accept all the shit that is thrown at them, and come back grinning for more. It makes me sick.' I asked him if he felt the same about the women. He thought for a moment. 'No. I admire them, at least those I meet, but they're all in the whoring industry. They do their job well. I know a lot of guys who've fallen for the love and marriage and misery ever after. Not me. But they serve me OK. I've no complaints over that. In fact, if I'm honest, that's one of the reasons I don't leave. They've got a feeling for good sex. They deliver. But the rest of it, you can stick it.'

There are patterns in the relationships between Western men and Thai women; some of them quite predictable. The story of Vince is characteristic. He came to Bangkok because his marriage of 25 years had ended. 'I thought that was the finish of my life. I could see myself getting older, in a bedsit with gas fire and second-hand furniture, milk bottle on the table, a packet of bread, crumbs in the marge. I knew about Thailand from a friend of mine I'd worked with who'd been stationed here.' (Vince worked as a sales representative for a British armaments manufacturing company. He says, 'I'm not proud of it, and I'm not ashamed either. I didn't make the world, I just have to survive in it.')

I came as a sex tourist. I'm not ashamed of that either. I didn't expect anything, except to screw my way out of being unhappy. I never imagined the women would be so different. I came to Pattaya, and it was like creatures from another planet. Out of this world. I think it was the third or fourth girl I met, something just clicked, and before I knew what had happened, I was in love with her. I gave her everything. It's a funny thing, but I never knew her real name. I just knew her as Pik. After 25 years with one woman, the last ten of them hell, I was dead sure I would never fall in love again. But I did, and that was within about a month of being here. I had quite a bit of money, and she did well out of me. I met the family, I bought them a pick-up truck so they could do the markets around Korat, they dealt in clothing, blouses, skirts, jeans. She could have had more. In a way, she wasn't ambitious enough. I guess she already had more out of me than her wildest imaginings.

For the first few months, I was in a kind of fever over her. Other people could see the warning signs. But I had no real friends here, you get mates by chance, because you're all here looking for the same thing and you're all in the same boat. I had drinking friends. If I'd been at home, I would never have caught fire like I did. I was not myself, that's all I can say. I was out of my social environment, and everything was more intense, more real. Actually, it was less real, but you find that out later. You suspend disbelief. I didn't look at the downside, because I didn't want to.

It wasn't till I got sick that I realised. I got a bad attack of malaria, I'd been to Vietnam for a holiday, and I was ill. And she never came. I kept thinking, 'She never got my letter, John never posted it.' I wrote to her again. I paid somebody to go up to Korat to see her. Still she didn't come. I realised she had dumped me. I was badly hurt. I loved her, boy, and when you love somebody in your fifties, don't you believe it when people tell you you don't feel like you do at 20. It's worse, you're more vulnerable, you're more desperate, you know it's the last throw.

I know now that's the way it is. They're doing a job. And their job is to get what they can. I don't hate her. I feel hurt. I got into something deeper than I knew. I thought I could handle everything, I was in charge of my life.

Men come to Thailand with money, and this gives them a feeling of great power and strength. It is strange how many of them are transformed, in their own imagination, into victims: they, the conquerors, the invincible, wind up feeling they have been cheated, their 'innocence' taken advantage of, their good-heartedness exploited. It is a strange reversal of reality.

Of course, the great majority of men who come on sex tours do not get involved to the same extent. They have come purely for fun, and they perceive their holiday as time out from life; they set it apart from their working and domestic lives and this makes them less susceptible to the complications of those who come looking for a love relationship. Some of the short-term tourists are extremely insensitive to the women, and have little imaginative understanding of the people whose lives touch theirs. 'A shower, a shag and a shit, the three biggest pleasures in life', said one man with his mates in a King's Corner bar in Patpong. Most say they come here 'for the pussy', 'fuck and forget 'em', 'because there's no complications', 'because the women are a good lay', 'they know how to make you feel like a man', 'they're professionals, even those who aren't'. It is difficult to dent this macho exterior, particularly when you meet people in the bars, when they have been drinking, or in a group: it is hard to say whether they are assuming what they think is an obligatory and defiant male bluster because the setting calls it forth, whether they are expressing a real sense of who they are, or whether it is a way of forestalling feelings of guilt. Certainly, when you talk to people as individuals, even the most aggressive become more thoughtful, and are interested in the lives of the women who service them; but they feel that by giving a generous tip, 'treating them decently', they have acquitted themselves of any debt to them.

Sometimes, it seems, the whole of Patpong is theatre, where people take on roles which are stereotypes, but which offer the comfort of escape from more troubling daily uncertainties of longer-term relationships. In that sense, it is an escape, an escape into the fantasy of men-as-men and women-as-women, an uncomplicated distribution of roles which provide a refuge from life, because nobody has to step outside the prescribed exchanges and dialogues. By being in groups, they fortify each other against yielding to the other fantasies that ambush longer-term visitors – the seductive tenderness and promises doomed to remain unfulfilled. In fact, many of these said they came originally to Thailand with mates or friends; they were secretly attracted to whatever lay beyond the sexual pliability of the women and came back later on their own to explore this further. Some were doubtless attracted to the opportunity provided to play out sexist and racist stereotypes, which they could no longer get away with at home; but I hesitate to generalise, because in many of the people I met, there was a pain, a confusion and sometimes an aggressive bluster, which all suggested more complex motives and deeper, often inaccessible, feelings.

III

I met SID on the plane going to Thailand. A dapper man in his mid-sixties, he was wearing cream trousers, white shoes, a flowered shirt; the uniform of his time off, as it were. He told me he was going to see his 'Thai wife'. He also said he has an English wife, but she doesn't like holidays and refuses to go abroad.

In fact, she won't go anywhere. Getting bargains on the local market, a new cardigan or skirt, nattering with her friends over tea, that's her idea of living. It isn't mine.

I gave up a lot of things for her when we got married. I used to love opera, ballet. I had to give it up, because she couldn't stand the noise. I kept on the straight and narrow till I was sixty. I think that's long enough for anybody. I would never think of leaving my wife, but if anything happened to her, I'd come to live here like a shot. Since I met Pia, my life has changed completely.

I came here for the first time with my daughter, on holiday. I went out once or twice on my own, went to some bars, just out of curiosity. I saw Pia, who was serving the drinks. She wasn't on the catwalk any more. She was in her thirties and if anybody made her an offer, she wouldn't refuse, but she knew she couldn't compete with the young girls. I took to her right away. There was something about her that was different: she was mature.

Now I come two or three times a year, just for three weeks at a time. I live for my holidays. When I go home, I feel a little bit guilty. I might do some extra work around the house, dig the garden, decorate a room or something. But I've nothing to feel guilty about.

I write to her whenever I'm coming and she always comes down to the bar where we met. I've given her some money – I got redundancy from the factory where I worked: we made machines for cigarette manufacture and exported them all over the world. I got good severance pay when it closed down in the 1980s. I didn't tell my wife exactly how much I got, I wanted a bit for my own purposes. So I gave Pia enough to start up a smallholding in her village, some chickens, ducks, pigs, a few fruit trees. She can't do enough for me. They know how to make a man feel looked after. Squeezing the toothpaste onto the brush so it's waiting for you when you go into the bath-room in the morning, that's what I call caring. How many women in England would do that?

Once I came and she wasn't there. I was disappointed. And angry. I said to the other girls in the bar 'Is there anybody who will take care of me till Pia gets here?' She hadn't got the letter or something. One girl, about 19, volunteered. I couldn't do anything with her. She was very sweet, but it would be like my own granddaughter. When Pia came, she was crying. She said to me, 'If you do that again, you will not see my love any more.' But she got the point. She's always been there on the dot, ever since.

You only have one life and if you go through it without doing anything, going anywhere, seeing the world, you might as well not have lived. So I'm happy. It suits me. I've left my wife comfortably off if anything happens to me. I don't think I'm doing any harm to anyone else, so why should I feel guilty? I mean, we should all have a conscience, but as long as nobody suffers, why should I make an issue out of it?

Those who were schooled to discipline and self-control in their youth, only to find that the world has turned upside down since then and that the most pressing necessity now is for people to get what they want, are well represented among sex tourists. Some are quite explicitly 'making up for lost time' and when they look back on their sexual abstinence and self-denial, they feel cheated and angry; as though the values of the present have robbed their past life of meaning, with its rigidly timetabled labour and even a personal life that now appears regimented and over-controlled. To make good a deficit of 'fun', sex and enjoyment is what many admit to coming to Thailand for; and however understandable this may be, it still leaves the agents of their late liberation – the women – in the dark as to the shadowy roles they are playing in these efforts to move with the times. There is another level of misunderstanding here; and a poignancy which undermines simple ideological interpretations that men with power are simply playing out their fantasies on powerless women. There is, of course, truth in that, but it is not, and never can be, the whole truth.

Indeed, many sex tourists, travellers to Thailand are no

longer from the more privileged sections of Western society. Some are now 'rednecks', racists, know-nothing adventurers, out simply for fun. Occasionally such people are caught carrying drugs into the country; they often behave in ways that are offensive and disparaging to Thai people. I met young men, who have come in groups, convinced that they 'know how to give Thai women what they want', unlike the 'wimps and poufs' which they perceive Thai men to be. It is a sad joke that such young men really believe that those Thai women they meet – mostly sex workers – are also looking for 'fun', rather than doing what, for a majority of them, is arduous and repetitive labour ...

But all social classes do come from the West to Thailand: businessmen, academics, executives too. Sex tourism, it seems, is a great leveller.

I met Alastair at a hotel where I was staying for a few days. A man in his fifties, he had come from Australia, when his contract with a university department was not renewed after 20 years. He had sued for wrongful dismissal, but the case was settled out of court and he was offered generous compensation by the university. At the same time, his marriage of more than 20 years had broken down.

He is a quiet, introspective man, who analysed his feelings and responses in a way that most did not. A small man with greying hair, rimless glasses and a slightly nervous manner. We shared some beers and, during the course of our conversation, he described the doubt and disillusionment he had experienced, after the initial euphoria of arriving in Thailand.

I was very elated when I first 'discovered' Thai women. It was such a relief to find people who don't ask questions. With my wife, for 20 years it had been, 'Do you love me, do I love you, how much do you love me, how much do I love you, is it enough; how good is our sex life, how bad is it, why did the magic go out of our lives, let's go for counselling, can we save our marriage, what about sex therapy?'

She was in therapy for six years and all she learned was that we had stopped loving each other. She spent a lot of money to find out the obvious. Actually, for many years, our relationship became the principal subject of all our conversations. It was like a third person, maybe the child we never had. But it sort of sat there, between us, crying for our attention.

At first I came for a vacation and I liked it so much that I came for six months, then another six months. I teach English, private students, so it is not all expense. I pay 300 dollars a month rent for a small room, with shower, air conditioning and TV. It is quite comfortable, good value.

I couldn't get over it. I went to the bars and I was completely dazzled by the ease of it, the apparent lack of hang-ups and not a mention of relationships! I met quite a few women. Some I stayed with only for a few weeks. I took Lin-Lin to Chiang Mai and went to Ubon with Oy to visit her family. It cost me a small fortune, but I didn't mind. I felt it was all for the pleasure of the moment. I lived a kind of hedonism I'd never known with Gemma, my wife. I thought we have become so self-conscious in the West, why can't we just get on with living instead of talking about it all the time? In Thailand, it seemed, relationships were something that happened, not another subject for academic investigation or psychotherapy.

It took almost a year before I noticed the other side of it. You see, the habit of analysing things doesn't go away – you take it with you; for about a year I'd kept it on hold, which was some achievement. I think now that was the happiest year of my life.

But I began to regret that nothing seemed to last. I wanted to set up some girl in an apartment with me, but she never seemed suitable, I thought it would never work out. I had learned some Thai, not a lot and we never had much to say to each other. I've seen tourists at breakfast in the hotels with their girls from the night before, reading the Bangkok Post, yawning, bored out of their skulls; or being trailed around department stores to go 'shopping'. I think the girls prefer the company of the other girls. When they are together, they are always much more animated and interested in what they're talking about, even though it might be just the strange habits of the latest farang. To live as a sex object must be terribly boring. I know many women like to hear how beautiful they are, how loving and wonderful, but I guess it gets a bit repetitive in the end.

Maybe if I'd had more money it might have made a difference. But I was on a limited budget and I've always been careful over spending. Some of the women could be terribly extravagant, as though they wanted to get as much out of you as they could before the spell wore off. Often sex was great, but in the morning, I sensed that we were both grateful to get away from each other. After one week, a month, they would leave and it was with a sense of relief that we parted. But that only meant I was free to start looking for the next one. You felt that the whole world was full of exciting new encounters and the only thing keeping you away from them was the woman you happened to be with at the moment.

I might have a couple of bad days, thinking, 'What the hell am I doing here, in this vile city in this foreign country?' But then, some stunning 22-year-old would appear, who behaved as though I was her man on a white horse. I do believe they think of their fathers when they meet mature men; and that's why they can be nice to them – to us, I should say. One day, a girl even called me Grandpapa and I didn't mind.

They changed me quite a bit; and I'm grateful for that. I'm by nature quite a mean person and I did learn to be more generous than my instincts would dictate. I think, 'I have more than they do, why not?' At first, delight in their company made me generous. But it got so that I started to look forward to the end of an affair, simply so I could get on with the next one. I resented whoever I happened to be with, because she was keeping me from all the other possibilities that were lurking round the next corner, whatever they might have been.

That went on for over three years. After a time, you've seen it all. You recognise the pattern and you come to see that is all it is – a pattern, with nothing behind it. It all just happens; as though Thai women are programmed to be what men want. In the end, you are not there as a person. You're just another shadow in their lives, one that coughs up the money. It is as though you do not reach them at all. What they are doing, they are doing with their bodies; certainly not their heart, certainly not their mind and not their spirit. This means you are involved with only a fraction of their being. I

think there is something about them that is inviolable; and
that is why they don't mind doing sex. It doesn't compromise the core of them. They have a kind of purity, which I
think only drives Westerners more crazy because we can't
understand it. I think for us, sex has become the essence of
life. That is a Western error and we project it on to everybody else in the world: if it's sex, it must be authentic; and
that is not necessarily true of sex in Thailand. Projection –
that's the secret of it. We see what we want to; but we are
not coming anywhere close to the reality of Thai women;
and that is both stimulating and ultimately, frustrating.

The predictability of everything here has become tedious.
I would watch her, fascinated, as she gazed at some invisible
speck on her cheek. Oy used a magnifying mirror so that she
could concentrate on the details of her face which were,
admittedly, lovely. But the mirror made even the pores in
the skin look like craters. The obsession with appearances
had a horrible effect on me. I realised that the feelings were
also like that – manicured, on show; the smile was an
aspect of cosmetics. One day, I observed it very keenly. I
was with Oy, just before she went home to her family for a
few days. I had been with her for about two months and I'd
been up there with her; not very far, just beyond Ayutthaya.
I had been a couple of times, very boring. Just drinking Thai
whisky and smiling till your jaw felt it was breaking. That
day, when I said goodbye to her, she turned off just a fraction too soon. I saw in her face that I no longer existed
when she was not with me, even while she was still half-
looking at me. Before she turned away, I just saw a blank
where I had been. Whenever we met, it was OK, because
her face would light up like a Christmas tree; the timing was
impeccable.

It hit me very hard: to see it in their eyes that you are
nothing in their lives. Their family, that is what exists. You
are only a means to that end. At the time I thought, 'You
ungrateful bitch', but inside, I was chilled to the bone. It was
like dying and the person who seemed closest to you not
caring. She really existed for me, but I didn't for her – that
was the difference.

After that, I never made another attempt to make a relationship. You see, I use the word that I thought I was

running away from when I finished with Gemma. Uncon-
sciously, I had been looking for a replacement of what I
thought I had turned my back on. What I got was a series of
beautiful exteriors, painted lacquer boxes with nothing inside.

Thais and relationships mean one thing – family. I saw
myself at that moment for what I was, one more punter,
another source of income, a casual employer. She'd done her
duty and more. That day, I saw her going off duty, clocking
out. If she had put her card in the factory time-puncher, it
could not have been more clear.

I guess I'm wiser now. Not sadder, because losing illu-
sions is a good thing. So why do I stay on! Why! Thai
culture is very seductive. That is its main characteristic. You
stay to be perpetually seduced, even if you know that
betrayal follows seduction as surely as night follows day. But
at least the women do take the trouble to seduce you, which
is a damn sight better than the wham, bam, thank-you-
Ma'am of Australia or America. The women have a skill ours
don't have; and that is what you're paying for.

You come from Australia or wherever, thinking that you are
escaping from the obsession with money, only to find you're
caught up in somebody else's marketing strategy. It's just that
they are selling dreams of sweetness in a sour, bitter world. I
guess I'll go on buying, but at least now I know what I'm
buying. When I see all these tourists going crazy over some bar
tramp, I quite enjoy it, thinking 'You'll learn'.

One of the most touching and successful stories I heard
between foreigners and sex workers came from Tony, now in
his sixties, originally from a town in Illinois in the American
Midwest. He met Nok 14 years ago, when he came to Thailand after the sudden death of his wife. He is plump, comfortably dressed in brown suede shoes and a linen jacket;
silver hair, a fleshy face with a pleasant smile.

It was the last thing I was looking for. I came for a vacation
just six months after my wife died. I came to get away from
the painful memories, which I just couldn't shake off, while
my daughter was selling the house. I didn't want to be there
any more. Grace, my wife, had not been sick. She was ill for
just two weeks before she died. She had cancer. There had

*been no warning, no pain. It just came out of the blue. She
had pains in her stomach one day and within a couple of
weeks she was dead. My beautiful wife.*

*I came on a tour of the Far East as a distraction. I had been
a junior executive in an insurance company, but I didn't want
to carry on. I just gave up everything. I didn't care if I lived or
died. I was going on an extended tour, but I got no further than
Bangkok. I went into some bars, but I didn't feel like sex. I
bought some girls a drink, talked to them about my wife,
which was not what they wanted to hear. They were sympathetic, but as soon as they realised I wasn't looking for consolation, they lost interest and went to sit in the lap of some
Japanese men who were. Then one night, Nok caught my eye.
She was more mature than the young women. Very sad face.
She had been a bar girl, but was now forty. She was, to my
mind, very beautiful. None of the other girls could match her. I
don't think the punters had shown much interest in her for
years. But I realised that young women were not what I
wanted.*

*I didn't approach her for two or three days. Every time I
went back though, she was there. When I told one of the
other girls I wanted to talk to her, she said, 'What? She is an
old woman.' I insisted. 'You can't. She just washes the
dishes.' They were amazed. The whole damn bar came to a
standstill. They watched us walk out together. I had this
funny feeling – the whole bar couldn't believe its eyes. There
was all this sweet young pussy in the place and this farang
comes in and makes for the oldest woman there.*

*I was certainly not going to fall for some young thing who
would be nothing but trouble. Nok thought she was past it;
but for my money, she is the sweetest, most attractive
woman in the world. She isn't Grace, that is the worst thing
I can say about her. I haven't spent a fortune on her, but I
gave her the money to start a food stall; that was her only
ambition.*

*I went to her village. She had two kids staying with the
grandparents. I visit once a year, stay maybe two months,
maybe three. There is no sign of any other man in her life. I
don't believe there is. She says I'm her husband. Whether
there is somebody else who disappears whenever I come I
don't know and I don't care. The place where she lives is*

still pretty primitive, an eight-hour bus ride. It's in another world. We sleep on the floor, a bedroll on some plastic stuff on concrete. There's cockroaches, mosquitoes. I'm happy. She cooks Thai food, which I love.

I love her because she understood instinctively about Grace. She didn't say she would try to take her place or anything like that. She just listened. I don't know where she learned her English. In fact, I don't know if she understood half of what I said. But that doesn't matter either.

My daughter does not approve. She came here once, six years ago. Never again. It was a disaster. She accused me of being unfaithful to her mother. I had known Grace since I was a kid – her father and mine had worked in the same place. She was a beautiful woman and a loving companion. I said to my daughter, 'You cannot be unfaithful to the dead.' Grace wouldn't have wanted me to mourn her for the rest of my life. So that has created a coolness with my daughter and her husband, but that's their problem. She doesn't say it, but she thinks Nok is just after money. Not that I have a great deal of it, but in Thailand, I guess, it's something. If there's any left when I die, Nok will have it. No question. She has tried to teach me Thai and I've tried to teach her more English. We didn't get very far, but it doesn't matter. The heart has a language all of its own.

We have a great friendship. Sex, yes, that's there. I don't know how to say this, but it's sleeping with her I like best. Sleeping. Holding. She winds herself round me as if we were teenagers. She cries when I leave and so do I. She always comes to meet me. I don't think there is anybody else. I don't know what her past life was and it is not important to me.

She has made my life sweet in my fifties and sixties and now at 66 I'm grateful. And I think she is grateful to me. I did kind of get her out of the bar. We go back there occasionally. Most of the girls who knew her have gone. It's a short life in those places. One or two have AIDS, some are married, some who are now older are working like Nok used to. Some have become domestic workers, others work for cleaning companies. It is sad to see what has happened. When we are young, we are very arrogant. We think it will last for ever.

Nok says she is very lucky, but I'm the lucky one. I don't want to hear any crap about Bangkok being sex and sleaze and all the rest of it. You can find happiness anywhere in this world and wherever it is, that place is holy. I thank God for her and I just wait for the time to come when I'll see her again. I say to my wife, to Grace that is, 'You don't mind, do you sweetheart?' And she doesn't. Wherever she is, she sure doesn't.

I won't take Nok to America. I thought about it, but no. She has her family here. Her children are married – they are more accepting of me than my daughter is of Nok. To me, Thailand is the place where I found some consolation for a loss I thought I could never bear. That's about it, I guess.

He looks up from his drink. His eyes, pale blue, fill with tears. One trickles down his cheek. He wipes it with his knuckles, like a child. 'Shit', he says, 'I'm telling you how happy she makes me and it makes me want to cry.'

IV

Andre, in his late sixties, is gay. Of French–German parents, he grew up in the Netherlands. He lives in a well-appointed condo in a street just off Sukhumvit. His sitting-room is full of Thai and European antiques, in which he has been a dealer for most of his life. There is a polished parquet floor, real leather sofa and chairs. Andre has been in Thailand for 25 years. He has organised his life with unusual foresight and intelligence, although he insists this was never done as an intellectual calculation. It was, he says, a response of the heart, although this was achieved only after some bitter experience.

All these farangs who arrive in Bangkok with a suitcase, they see some pretty boys and girls and they think love is theirs for the asking. They think a young man or woman will whisk them away to a life of pleasure and enjoyment. It is an impossible dream they come with, and it is always doomed to disappointment. Some of them take a boy or a woman to Europe or America; there, the boy falls in love with a woman or the woman falls in love with someone of her own age. So they become angry, put them on a flight back to Thailand. This has happened to so many people. They act without thinking about the consequences.

I learned to separate my need for sex from my need for

love. When I was younger, in Holland, I fell in love with a gypsy boy; and he stayed with me for ten years. That is, he remained my friend. He was 16 when I met him, but he was already physically an adult. One day, his mother came to my flat with him, and she admonished him in front of me, 'You go only with this man. He will look after you.' They lived in a caravan; they were very poor. He came to see me two or three times a week. But of course, when he came to be 19, 20, he wanted a girl. One evening, he came to me and he said, 'I'm just going out for a cup of coffee. I'll be right back.' And I knew immediately what he meant. We had that kind of understanding that he did not need to spell it out and I did not need to press him to find out the details. He turned to me and smiled, and he knew that I knew. I wrote a poem about it: A Cup of Coffee.

But it was a shock to me; I had not thought it would be like that. But I knew I had no choice but to accept. And of course, that was right. There would have been no point in making some kind of scene, of being jealous. He remained my friend for ten years, and I learned many things from that boy.

I have very particular tastes. I like a boy to be 18; not 17, not 19. This is something very precise, while they are poised between adolescence and manhood. I very quickly learned that if I tried to prolong such relationships, they would not work. It may last for two or three years, but there is no future in it. So I learned that the only way to deal with this problem was to keep the two things separate. But then the question remained, how did I deal with my need for love and affection? Well, I adopted boys. And the boys I adopted I would never dream of touching. My need for paternity and fatherly affection was very strong, and I had no difficulty in separating this from my need for sex.

The first boy I adopted was from Morocco. His father was killed in the Agadir earthquake. Under Muslim law, you cannot adopt, so I had to wait till he was 21 before I could do it legally. He is a Berber. He now runs a café in Brussels and is married to an Algerian girl. They have two children. They say to me 'Papa, why do you not come and live with us all together here?'

The second was a Dutch boy. He was living in an orphanage. His father was a drinker who committed suicide.

I adopted him legally; in fact, I was the first male to adopt a child in Holland. The case made history. Everything was done legally.

I adopted my Thai son here in Thailand. You can't do this now, but you could then. His father was also a drinker. The family had no time for the boy. I went to his home village, received permission from the parents. I went to the local authority, went through all the formalities in order to make it legal.

I gave Dutch citizenship and my name to all three. When they were younger – all were children when I adopted them – I would travel round and take them with me to stay in hotels. Reception would sometimes phone and say, 'A boy has come who wants to go to your room; please send him down.' I could then take the passport and show them my name and say to them 'Now you understand?' I do not care what people think. I knew what I was doing and it was something good. I never had any sexual relationship of any kind with the boys I adopted.

It is as though you have a garden. You have to plant trees and nurture them. At first, they will not bear fruit, but later, they may; even then, you cannot be certain that they will. I am now living with my Thai son and his wife. They have a baby, ten months old, whose name means Dust. He is a beautiful child and I am very happy. I take care of them and they look after me. I enjoy my family life.

This is what many gays do not understand. Either they do not believe me when I say I never had sex with those I adopted or they think I am crazy. Many gays are very selfish. They have never had to place the interests of another human being before their own, never known what it is to look after children first. The only thing they think of is taking care of their own desires.

This is why it is better if, like me, you prefer boys who are not gay. You may become friends with them, but inevitably, one day, they will go off and find a girl. So if you expect them to love you, you are making a serious mistake. You will always be disappointed. If you take a boy who is gay, he will always want to go and find someone of his own age. If he is pretty, he will run around and give you nothing but pain. I do not want this; in fact, I wish to avoid it.

But here in Thailand, a boy who is not gay will give you sex. I have one who visits me once a week. He is 18; he will come three times in the space of two hours. These boys are not conscious of age in the way that gays or Europeans are. In Europe, if you are 30 and you go into a gay bar, they will look down on you, as if to say 'What are you doing here, at your age?'

Gays are like this. I had two American friends here. They are 70 now, but they have been friends since they were kids. One day, when they were 16, they were in some public toilet in America and a 21-year-old came in and offered them 2 dollars for sex. They looked at him and said, 'What, with you?' He was already too old for them at 21. I say to my gay friends, 'Go and look in the mirror and think of what you see. Do you think any gay boy will go with you for anything but money?' They come here and think they are going to be loved. They find a certain difference here, a sweetness and they think it is love. They have to learn and some do so only after the most painful experiences, disappointments, betrayals. They think they can buy love or friendship, but they can do neither. These things are not on the market and never will be; but counterfeits are there. Not the real thing.

I did not make a self-conscious effort to do this. But I knew in my heart that I had to make my own dispositions, make the arrangements necessary for the satisfactions I require in life. My children love me. I chose their wives for them. The Dutch boy, he married a Japanese girl, but the marriage broke down and he returned to Holland. He became a drinker, like his father. He is now a dealer in second-hand furniture from sales and auctions. I was – and remain – a dealer in high-class antiques. That is how I made the money that has enabled me to do what I do. His is a very small-time business. There is something of his father in him.

Andre shows me photographs of his children; as they were when they were children, as they were growing up, as they are now. He says: 'I don't say love does not exist between an older and a younger man. But it is very rare when it is not for money. It is the same with women. It can happen, but in general, it doesn't. So the people who come to Thailand do so suspending disbelief. That means they want to think that the woman or the boy loves them for themselves and not for their money. The two Americans I was talking about said, "Yes, that is right; we knew each other at 16 and we still see each other as we were then. We do not feel our age. Only others see it. We should learn to see it ourselves." Many of these gay men who have never had responsibility see themselves still as children.'

When I was in Bangkok in April 1995, there was a story in the Thai papers of two Dutchmen who had been caught in a hotel bedroom with two boys, one 17, the other 13. The penalty in Thailand for having sexual relations with a boy of 13 is ten years imprisonment; with a 17-year-old, it is two or three years. There was a picture in *Thai Rath*, the paper with the widest circulation in Thailand: an elderly man wrapped in a towel, a boy sitting on the bed, eyes lowered in shame. The man with the younger boy paid the police 10,000 US dollars to get his passport back, the one with the older boy 4,000 dollars. The police took the money and the two men returned to their own country without charges being made against them; the only penalty being the financial one exacted by police private enterprise. Andre says of these men: 'They are foolish. It is not sensible to break the law of the country where you stay. To be a pedophile is a terrible thing. They need compassion, but they cannot be allowed to do this with children. I love my children and one's instinct is always to protect them. If my son found out that anyone had touched his child, he would throw that person over the balcony from the eighteenth floor, without stopping to wait for explanations. There is a farang living in a building near here, who always has 13- and 14-year-olds visiting him. He is asking for trouble. One day he will be caught by the authorities or killed by the father of one of the boys. Why people take such risks I do not understand.'

Bernard Trink is a writer with the *Bangkok Post*, a long-term observer of the bar scene and a controversial columnist. He has lived in Bangkok for 25 years, chronicling the encounters of farangs with Thailand and the misapprehensions and cross-cultural difficulties that arise from them. He originally came as a visitor and stayed because he preferred the pace of life here over that of his native New York. The contrast is now less great and Bangkok is increasingly adopting the tempo of any other metropolis.

He married a Thai woman and they have three children. He is, he insists, untypical, in that he married someone from 'respectable society', the daughter of a naval officer. The stability of his own marriage has made him a wry and sometimes curiously idiosyncratic observer of foreigners, many of whom come here on short visits and forge relationships and contract marriages that cannot last. He has a good deal of sympathy for the women in the sex industry, but his view is coloured by a cynicism which many women resent.

Even if there are 300,000 prostitutes in Thailand, which is my reckoning, that is still only one per cent of the women in the country. That is not a significant proportion of the population, contrary to the popular image of Thailand. Of course, that figure involves certain women who enter and leave the work after only a short time. And there are those who are not averse to earning a little extra money, maybe garment workers and other industrial employees who can always be procured for customers who prefer such girls.

The working life of the women is short. Generally, they are finished by the age of 29–31. There are always younger girls coming in, so they are well aware when their time is coming to an end – they do not get taken off from the bar so often, their income dwindles. It is very competitive, a very crowded market.

Many of the women enjoy the limelight of admiration. When she is on stage, wearing a bikini, or nothing at all, she exults in her own desirability, she feels the elation of being wanted. It is no use denying this, it is real. It also becomes addictive, very hard to do without. And the social life with the other women is very important; banter and chat and support and comparing experiences. So if a farang comes and takes her off to some hotel, it is OK for a short time, but in a little while, she will hanker after the sheer excitement and fun of the bars.

Even if she marries a farang and goes to live abroad, she will feel restless after some time. She will want to come back to Thailand to see her sick mother. And her husband will say 'OK, go for two or three weeks.' And she does go to see her sick mother, spends at least one night with her. Then it's straight back to the bar to resume the life she had, find the admiration she enjoyed once more. Then she'll go back to her husband, be the model wife until next year. But when she's married, she ceases to get the feeling of delight in her desirability that she was used to. She must now do the cooking and shopping and washing. She probably thought that all these things would be taken care of by servants, as they would be for rich people in Thailand, but she soon finds it's her job. But for the sake of the security her position gives her, she will put up with it.

A lot is said about the dependency of the girls' families on the money they send home. In my experience, if they do send any, it isn't much. Often they don't. They buy clothes, TV and video and many are gamblers, playing cards or mah-jong. Sometimes, fantastic amounts of money pass through their hands. But the idea that they are doing it for the family, that they become prostitutes for the greater good, is a convenient alibi. And they will indeed send something home, what they have left over. But then, you don't have to send very much to keep a family in rice twice a day – a few hundred baht a month is no hardship to them. The family are happy; so everybody can be satisfied. But it is mainly a fiction, to touch the hearts and pockets of farangs.

The girls see the foreign visitors as an opportunity. They perceive them as greedy, on the make, looking for something for nothing. They do not see themselves as making a relationship with the farang, nothing lasting, just some fun and some money. They might get to spend time in a luxury hotel, but they know this is not their real life. They are opportunistic. They believe they cannot trust the farangs. They know how to behave prettily, to be affectionate. Then sometimes the farang gets hooked. He falls in love with her. When he asks her to marry him and she says yes, he can't believe his good luck. He's got it all.

But most of the young women are migrants to Bangkok, from the North or the Northeast. A few are local girls, but the majority have come from up-country. The relationship often does not last. They are, after all, prostitutes. It is their job. This is when the farang gets disillusioned and starts accusing them *of false promises, of leading them on. It is a cultural misunderstanding. They say yes to the marriage proposal, because they know Thai husbands won't be faithful; there is just a chance that the farang will. There are, of course, happy marriages. Mine is. But these are the exception. The kind of people who become prostitutes are a particular kind of person. That is as true of Thailand as of any other country. So to fall in love with one of them is to court certain risks. Lies, illusions, faking – it is all part of the business.*

I was interviewed not long ago by a New Zealand TV crew about some Thai prostitutes in New Zealand. They wanted me to talk about Thailand as a country of prostitution. 'Why do they do it?' they asked. I said 'For the money, the same as New Zealand prostitutes do.' 'But why Thais?' they insisted. I said 'Look, I can show you New Zealand girls who are working for escort agencies in Bangkok. You want to meet them?' I don't think the programme was ever shown.

When the women leave the industry, most have some little savings and they will find some other occupation to invest it in – a small grocery store, a hairdressing shop or beauty parlour in the village, vegetable or fruit-vending in Bangkok. They still have a long life ahead of them. Many already have one or more children before they even come to the city. They leave them with grandparents or neighbours. Some of these children later come to Bangkok to follow the same business: a new generation is already here now. Sometimes, a whole group of girls come from one particular village; so links between certain communities are created.

When I first came, Patpong was all small businesses and shops. Little by little, they were bought out and opened up as bars. There is no mafia, only local business people. It is said that the Vietnam war created prostitution when Bangkok became a rest and recreation facility. There were over 70,000 men in the city at any one time. But it existed in Thai society long before the Americans came. All the Americans did was to bring sex and music together – they started the bar culture by integrating sex with music.

Now we see more and more massage parlours opening up, which also have cubicles, where varying degrees of sexual activity can take place. This is just another step of integrating everything under one roof. Until now, bars have only been places from where people take the girls off and take them to hotels.

Some of Bernard Trink's views are more eccentric. Of the AIDS issue, he says he thinks it has been

blown up out of all proportion. It is a scare, a moral panic that has now become big business. There are at least 25 different conditions that will show up in tests as HIV-positive, illnesses where the immune system has been weakened. These include malaria, TB, malnutrition, even flu. HIV does not lead inevitably to AIDS. The AIDS virus lives 20 seconds outside the body. It is not easily transmissible through heterosexual intercourse. Homosexuals get it more easily through anal intercourse because that tears the muscle of the sphincter. But with heterosexual relationships, there is no such damage. It is natural, there is rarely blood, the natural lubrication of the body ensures that.

Listen, these girls are screwing their brains out five or six nights a week. There is no evidence of AIDS in Patpong. It is not a pandemic, as those who have a vested interest in spreading fear would have us believe. For ten, twelve years, they have been saying 'It is coming', but it is always the apocalypse tomorrow. Now some so-called experts are saying it can remain 20, even 40 years in the body before it becomes AIDS. Well, people are going to die of old age, in car accidents, of pollution and heart attacks before then. If all they say is true, we would have expected to see many more dying in Patpong. It has not happened. Of course, you start plying people with AZT, that will certainly destroy the immune system. You have a 'cure' that is actually spreading the disease. Normal sexual activity does not produce AIDS in my opinion. But such are the vested interests, the power of doctors, of pharmaceutical companies, the armies of instant experts, that you cannot go against the prevailing wisdom.

This is one of the reasons why I maintain a non-judgemental attitude to the sex scene in Bangkok. If what has been predicted were remotely true, we should by now be in the grip of a major epidemic. Look at the plague in the fourteenth century – that wiped out half of Europe. The Spanish flu in the 1920s killed 20 million. We have seen nothing like that. I don't know how anyone claims to know statistics – there are officially some 6000 AIDS patients in Thailand – that is a far cry from the doom-laden prophecies of the last few years; and these are mainly intravenous drug users, homosexuals and those who've had transfusions of contaminated blood.

Many groups working with women and with AIDS-prevention programmes do not share this optimistic view of the issue. Siriporn Skrobanek, of the Foundation for Women, says that because there are continuous screenings of the women in Patpong and in the areas of high-profile international sex tourism, as soon as a woman is diagnosed HIV-positive, she will lose her job. She knows no other work, has no other skills. Naturally, she will drift towards the cheaper brothels, karaoke lounges or restaurants, where the owners are less punctilious about the state of health of their employees. These cheaper places are likely to be frequented by Thai people – especially migrant labourers, construction and factory workers. They become infected and when they return to their villages, they will infect their wives and ultimately, their unborn children. In some parts of the North of Thailand, the number of HIV-positive pregnant women has reached 7 per cent. This is how the highly visible transnational part of the sex industry is kept 'clean' and 'respectable'. Those who pay the price for this are, not for the first time, the weakest and most vulnerable people in society.

What has been predicted *is* happening; it is simply that it has been spirited out of sight of the gaudy bars of Patpong and Pattaya. Tourism – of which sex tourism is a significant component – makes far too lucrative a contribution to the Thai economy for it to be jeopardised by the fate of the poorest.

There are other factors which help to preserve the image of the international bars: in many, the management is sufficiently enlightened to allow the women to refuse customers who will not use a condom. There is a more sophisticated awareness of the issue and this inhibits the spread of HIV in the higher reaches of the commercial scene. But this does not mean that the scare is false. Nor, of course, does it mean that AIDS cannot be a consequence of 'normal' intercourse, as experience in many parts of Africa has shown.

V

Frank is in his mid-seventies. He had a suburban childhood in South London. His father was a City of London banker, and he went to Dulwich College, and then into the Royal Air Force during the Second World War. In 1944–45 he was in Rangoon. Frank says that at that time there was much covert homosexuality in the services; the authorities both knew and chose not to know. As long as you were not caught, it was OK. It was considered an expression of comradeship, it was 'what lads sometimes did when they had beer inside them'.

I desperately tried to deny it to myself. I thought it was just part of growing up, and it would pass. But it didn't. The others were just playing around. For me, it was serious. I went to a psychiatrist in Harley Street. He said to me, 'It's up to you. Either you go this way, and lead a normal life, or you go the other way, and bring disgrace to your family and finish up in the News of the World.' (A newspaper which specialised in salacious sexual court stories.) This man was supposed to have hypnotised me; he brought his cigarette close to my arm, and said 'You won't feel this'; but he never actually touched me with it.

I tried everything. I had these pictures, photographs of Arab boys. I cut off the top, the head part, and beneath them I placed images of women, female bodies. I thought, 'If I can start like that, imagine boys with women's sexual parts, little by little, I would change.' But I didn't.

In Calcutta, I went to a brothel. It was at the end of the war; a dark, murky place on Sudder Street. I think I was probably half drunk. I don't remember much about it; all I know is, it didn't make any difference.

When I came to recognise I was not going to change, I went to live in Denmark. Copenhagen then – it was the 1950s – was very much what Paris had been at the turn of the century. I worked for a bank as a translator from Danish into English. At that time, Denmark was still a predominantly rural society. With many poor migrants coming to the city, it was easy to get boys; and there was no law against it, as there was in Britain. But eventually, Denmark became like the rest of Europe. Prostitution became more organised, the people became harder and more money-minded, and you could no longer find affection. So around 1970, I shifted to Thailand. It was then very much as Denmark had been in the early 1950s.

But I've no friends here. I've lived in this hotel for seven years. Management are very good, I get concessionary rates. I think they are trying to raise the tone of the place a little, it has had a rather dingy reputation in recent years. When I first came here, there were two other Brits living here – one an old cricket umpire, the other a good friend, who committed suicide some years ago. I still miss him. I shall never get over that. We used to share so many things, a love of music, cricket, talk of home. Now I see virtually no one. They are kind to me here, but the smile you get is quite disproportionate to the service they render; it cannot be sincere. I've a boy who comes once a week. I've known him four years. He rarely stays more than an hour and all he wants is money and more money. He needs so much for the instalments on his motorbike, then he spends it before he can pay and then needs it all over again. He is rapacious.

The trouble is, I like straight boys and that's my problem. But you can't make relationships with them. When I walk out of this place, I don't speak a word to anyone. I don't speak much Thai. My life here is meaningless. You need someone to share the same interests. What I miss most is companionship, friendship, comradeliness, call it what you will.

I go back once a year for what I call Eurotherapy; at least there your assumptions are shared generally, you don't have to start from scratch in a strange culture you can never understand. I have a sister who lives in sheltered accommodation run by the Church in Bristol. I could go there. She would like me to. But it is so regimented, meals at fixed times, religious offices, some meals in silence. I've stayed very British, even though most of my life has been outside Britain. I can't change that, I'm too old to adapt now.

I sleep till eleven or so in the morning, then have breakfast. Not Thai food, I don't really like it. Then I fall asleep again in the early afternoon. My first drink is never before eight o'clock. Then I to to sleep early, unless I get involved

*in something on TV for an hour or two. I had an accident,
which has damaged one of my discs, so I am in constant
pain. I used to play the piano, but my fingers have become
stiff with arthritis, so I can't do that any more.*

When I was there, Frank was preparing to go home to England
for six weeks. It was early September. The rain had started in
earnest in Bangkok. Frank said: 'I dread going home, because
although I've a couple of friends there, I've no real life. I dread
it also, because I have to come back to this eventually. I'm
thinking of placing an ad in the paper here, offering English
conversation, just for the sake of the company; but if you do
that, you never know who will latch on to you. I don't like to
be disturbed, but I'm dying of boredom. It's a strange contra-
diction, loneliness and boredom. I don't know.'

I went to see Frank several times before he left. He was
always on the verge of cancelling his flight, of postponing his
visit to the UK; yet he couldn't leave it any later in the year,
because he dreaded the cold and rain of a London autumn.

Frank is 75, still youthful-looking, with clipped hair, a
square jaw; wiry, anxious, slim. Just before he left, he kept
checking his belongings, packing and unpacking items he
thought he might need. He said: 'I'm going home. At least,
that's what I say. The trouble is, I don't know what home
means any more. I've a Danish passport, I live in Thailand,
but I'm British to the core.'

Gerard is a pedophile, who vigorously denies there is anything reprehensible about his preferences. He spent much of
the time we spoke together justifying himself. He feels little
guilt, because his experience of what he desires is, to him,
positive. He appears to be angered and puzzled by the profound disapproval his conduct inspires.

Gerard is in his late thirties. I met him in the park and
we started a conversation because he was grateful to find
someone with whom he could speak French. Many people
are eager to talk; and it is enough not to contradict them, to
remain a shadowy and vaguely assenting presence for them
to tell you their life story; you have no substance for them,
you exist only as a repository for their sometimes burden-
some secrets.

Gerard gave a defensive account of why he sees no reason to curb his desire for 12- and 13-year-old girls. In fact, he says, he usually has to settle for older girls who look skinny and underdeveloped. There are, he assured me, even places where 18- and 19-year-olds deliberately cultivate a pubescent image to cater to particular tastes. (I had met such young women in Manila a few years before; they were elective anorexics, permanently malnourished, because in that way, they could offer themselves as perpetual virgins to foreign tourists.)

Gerard said there are many young girls available in Thailand 'if you know where to look for them'. I asked him what that meant and he became vague; afraid, perhaps, that I might be prising secrets from him. He said: 'The world is full of such girls, especially in the country areas.' He insisted that 'showing them kindness and affection is surely better than kidnapping them and selling them to the brothels. I detest this hypocrisy. I have never ill-treated a girl. In my country, children are regularly murdered, sexually assaulted and mutilated; it appears in the newspapers every day. I cannot understand why anybody would want to do this to a child. I love children. I never have sex with a girl if she does not want it also. People underestimate the sexual being of children, at least of some children. I don't say all children, because you develop an instinct, a recognition of those who are ready for it and those who are not; the latter one leaves alone. I would not violate a child of nine or ten; people who do that are disgusting.' (This appears to be another feature of those who break customary laws and taboos – they always focus on others who do worse things, who are more outcast, whose behaviour is more distasteful, so that they can contrast themselves virtuously from such 'monsters.')

There are girls here of 13, 14, some of whom have been in the sex industry for two years or more. How can they be damaged by me? I would like to look after them, to rescue them, take care of them. If it were possible, I would take them home, see that they are educated for some useful job. I would never take advantage of a girl.

You would be surprised how many girls actually initiate a sexual approach, and I am not talking of girls in the brothels.

Maybe that is the only way they know of asking for affection and love. Love is the most important thing. Sex is only a secondary manifestation of it. I was a teacher in France and I fell in love with many of my pupils. I loved them; but of course, as a teacher, I did not express any such feelings. But always, there were girls who would stay behind after the rest of the class had gone. There were girls who would behave provocatively. They knew what they were doing. Sex is no longer a mystery, a secret for children. They know of it from being quite small, and naturally, there are those who develop faster and there are also those who have an overwhelming need to be held and loved.

Ours is a very cruel society. In that school there were children who had been abused, emotionally, and sometimes physically, tortured and beaten. Some had been traumatised; and they were expected to sit down and do maths or learn English. Some parents were monsters to their own children. The teachers used to discuss it, but to them, it was part of the natural order of things. I was horrifed and disgusted by it. But if anyone had touched a child, even with loving, tender hands, there would have been such an outcry, not least from the parents who had been the most abusive and destructive; such a person would have been at the mercy of the lynch mob.

I say quite clearly that I do not see anything wrong with my desires. I believe that many 12- and 13-year-olds are quite capable of knowing what they want. Look at the number of girls in Western Europe who are pregnant at 13, 14. The boys are often 19 or 20. This is now more or less regarded as normal, a fact of life. Girls mature earlier. Yet I am to remain forever excluded from expressing what is natural to me and to thousands of other people in the world. I believe one day the prohibition on relationships with children will come to be seen as archaic as the laws against divorce or laws against homosexuality. I would never do anything against the girl's will. She has the right to choose her life, just as I do.

To every objection he had an answer. How, I asked, can a 12-year-old be equated with a mature adult? Surely, there can never be equality. He said: 'For one thing, how many adults are mature? And for another, many children are already old at 12. Many have seen and done things which shock me also. In Thailand, parents sometimes sell their daughters for the sake of a TV set or a new car; how can what I do be worse than that? I am seeking to protect her, not harm her.' I queried this concept of having a relationship with a 13-year-old by taking her somewhere, paying money and then leaving. How could that be an expression of love? 'This is because society will not permit such a relationship to develop openly and naturally', he replied. 'If I could choose, I would take just one girl and love her with all my heart.' I said, 'If you only like girls of this age, what happens when they become 14 or 15? Do you abandon them?' 'I don't know; I have never been permitted to discover. It could be that my love for her would grow with time and I would want to stay with her. I do not know. I am 38. It is not inconceivable that we would stay together, maybe even get married eventually. I don't know.'

Gerard was aware of his feelings for younger girls when he was adolescent.

When I was 15, I used to enjoy the company of younger girls. It was always the precocious ones who came to me. I knew even then that what people know about sex they conveniently forget later, in order to deny the sexuality of their children. But then I became ashamed and, for a long time, I just suppressed the feelings I had. When I became a teacher, there was a girl, she was 14. She always just chanced to meet me, in the corridor, on the street, in the shops. One day, I saw her close to the place where I was living. Her father was a drunk and her mother a prostitute. She was hungry, starved of affection. She was the first one; but it was not I who initiated it. She was already a young woman. I prefer the lean stringy girls, those who have not yet become fully female.

At one time, I thought I might be gay, but I'm not interested in boys or men. Or grown women. Sometimes I think there must have been something that happened to me as a child, maybe I am fixated in some way. I have a sister two years younger than me. I am very fond of her. We were very close and I can tell her everything. She does not judge me.

My father was a manager in a chemicals company. My mother was younger than him, a very stupid vain woman. He thought she was just waiting for him to form her, to shape her to his tastes and dispositions; but she remained vain and spoiled. Maybe there is something there. In a way, my mother is a kind of child, impetuous, wilful. She must have her way or she weeps and rages. No one can contradict her without provoking a storm. But she is detestable. I'm not saying that has anything to do with it because that sounds as though I am making excuses. What I want is the right to express my sexuality and that means also the right of children to have their sexuality recognised, right from the earliest years. Sex is as much part of the life of children as of adults. We deny it because it suits us to see them as innocents. Unfortunately, it works both ways – neither parents nor children can believe in each other's sexuality. They have to pretend it isn't there.

In Bangkok it is becoming difficult now. There are other places, where needy children are crying out for the affection of adults. I went to Cambodia, Laos, Vietnam – so many kids whose lives have been scarred by social disruption, war, violence, the destruction of families. I don't think I'm doing anything bad. I am offering a girl security in a cruel, insecure world. Such a big deal about sex. That isn't the most important thing. Love is.

Yet there is often inconsistency between the way people present themselves and the reality. Gerard later told me he had met one 13-year-old girl through a woman who claimed to be a relative of the child. This relative stayed with the girl in his house for six months, where she was supposed to be the housekeeper, while the girl shared Gerard's bed. He paid this woman a weekly allowance. 'She was a lazy slut. She did nothing. But in the end, she became very greedy, so I had to tell them both to get out. She threatened me, but since the aunt, or whoever she was, had been the main party to the deal, she had no option. They left and I never heard from them again.' I said that if he loved the child so much, it seemed to go against this love of children to make her pay for the aunt's greed. He became impatient and said 'Why are you judging me?' He refused to speak any more and walked away, offended.

VI

Heinrich is a former steel worker, now living in a suburb of Dusseldorf. He is of indeterminate age, with dyed fair hair, well built; perhaps in his fifties. I met him in a bar called King's Castle. He was rather drunk, and behaving belligerently towards some of the girls, who were avoiding him. He turned to me as someone to talk to. The conversation was in German, to a deafening thump of music. I don't think Heinrich even realised I was not German, which says much about the nature of the interaction, given my fairly basic understanding of German.

He was angry and aggressive; evidently wanted to talk about a woman he had met here. Without any preamble he said,

I gave her everything. I came here, and I picked her up, and she said she loved me. Why did I believe her? Why should I believe she would choose to love me, out of all the men she must have met? I spent money on her, thousands of marks.

When she wasn't with me, I thought she was at home with her family, or staying in her room. She was double-crossing me all the time. I was crazy for her. I wanted her all to myself. In the end I asked her to marry me. Not for love by then. For revenge. I took her back to Germany. I wanted her to work for me. She had used me to get money out of me, I thought 'Why should I not do the same?' I took her back and put her on the streets. Not on the streets exactly, we were more discreet than that. We stayed together. We rented a separate room where she could do the business.

When she got to Germany, she was scared, she couldn't speak the language. She was in my hands. But boy, was she good at her job. I didn't use any middlemen, none of this buying and selling whores. I could do it all by myself. In the end, she got good at it and could pretend to enjoy it. I figured that the skills she had in Thailand would go down very well in Germany. And they did. She was very much in demand. We were making big money. I got her to come on to the men there as she had come on to me in Bangkok. They fell for it. They parted with 1000 marks a night, 2000. They gave her presents. We moved into a bigger apartment.

We had a ball. I won't say she liked it, but she accepted it. This was her fate. This was her job.

But she met some guy she fell in love with. She told him she was working for me. I don't know how she put it, maybe she told him I was keeping her prisoner, she hated me. They fucked off together. One day, she was going to the club to work. She never came back. Maybe she's working for him now.

That's what I'm doing here now. I'm looking for another one. I got used to the life I was leading. I don't want to give it up. Exploitation is their game; but two can play.

Conrad Lorenz is a gay man of about 40 from Sri Lanka. He has been working as a journalist in Hong Kong for the past nine years. His mother has just been visiting him in Hong Kong, where she spent three weeks, and now he is taking a week off in Bangkok.

We were a mixture of Dutch, Portuguese, Celanese. I come from a privileged background. My father went to Oxford. Our culture was very anglicised. When he came back to Ceylon, as it then was, he had a nervous breakdown. My mother went to the Royal Academy of Music and became a music teacher. Our home language was English; and my Celanese is still not very good. I went to a posh English medium school and college. There was a bit of sexual horseplay there, but I never got involved with it, because I knew, even then, that for me it mattered too much.

I was actively gay as a young man in Sri Lanka, before the troubles. I had an attraction to military, police and naval uniforms, especially tight uniforms that moulded the contours of the body. I used to pick them up and take them home. In fact, on our verandah, when these military friends came, I realised that was the first time Celanese had ever been spoken there.

I was brought up a Catholic, my mother was Catholic, my father Anglican. We were part of a very distinctive community, and we had enjoyed considerable power and influence under the British. Since Independence, we have just sort of melted away. Many have gone to Australia. It is very sad. There is nothing there for me now. I got a job in Hong

Kong, but for the first six or seven years I hated it. As a dark-skinned man, I was well placed to judge the effect of Chinese racism. They were not racist to Westerners. I have an American friend and he gets as many sex partners as he wants. I think I went to Hong Kong partly to do penance for what I considered my sins. Certainly in Hong Kong, my sex life is negligible compared to what it is in Sri Lanka. My mother has known from when I was quite young, but I was always ashamed to tell my father. I wrote him a letter to tell him, and he sent for me; my mother and father were living separately at that time. He said it was OK; he had no adverse judgement. But I couldn't come out publicly. I did so a week after he died.

I hated both Westerners and Chinese at first, because Westerners got preferential treatment everywhere. I was made to feel the meaning of racism. People thought I was Indian. The most hated are the Indian traders, and I have to say they are not, on the whole, a very agreeable lot. So my sex life became more theoretical, aesthetic: I went to the pools and beaches and just looked at the beautiful bodies of the men. I think that young Chinese and Japanese males are the absolute perfection of human beings.

I don't like young people. I like those where the supple willowiness of youth has been tempered by discipline and control and whose bodies are firm from that discipline. My physical contact is minimal. It is a gayness of the spirit, a sense of beauty, a feast for the eyes. It has taken me some time to reach this position. At first, I just hated the exclusion. Now I love Hong Kong. I couldn't go back; the more so since I earn in a day what I would earn in a month in Sri Lanka. Hong Kong is a very hard city. I come to Bangkok to go to the baths, clubs, pay 1000 baht to a boy. I don't know if that is too much, I can't bargain with them. I spend a lot of money here. It gives me a kind of release I don't get in Hong Kong. Although there are bars and saunas now, sex in public places is still illegal under old British colonial laws.

I think the Chinese will allow Hong Kong to go on as it is for two or three years after 1997, then they'll clamp down suddenly. That's a very Chinese thing. Westerners are admired in Hong Kong. Western cultural and linguistic influence are weapons in the ideological war. The British have liberalised the social structures – a bit late with democracy – as a Trojan horse for China. This is their legacy to make the takeover harder, but they have not been quite smart enough; they left it all a little too late.

Japanese videos are my consolation in Hong Kong; they are so much more subtle and beautiful than American gay videos. The American ones are crude and exaggerated and leave nothing to the imagination.

I don't know what I'll do after 1997. I'll stay until it becomes intolerable. I don't know why I stuck it for so long when it was a continuous torment. I guess that is my Catholic heritage. But now I love it. I just have to come to Bangkok every few months for some relief. Smile, relaxed – deep I don't think it is. Chinese friendships are deep. Bangkok is a terrible place. In Hong Kong everything runs smoothly and efficiently. I was picked up by the police once in a sauna in Hong Kong; no doubt I'm on some computer. When I come here, it feels so free. I make the most of every minute because here, I can get all the things I can't at home.

I met an American in his forties who had picked up a young woman in one of the bars and gone back to the village near Chiang Rai in the North. There he had found himself attracted to the sex worker's mother.

She was a good woman. She had had seven children. Her husband had gone. She was a damn handsome woman, natural. She wasn't dressed up, she wasn't glamorous. I felt embarrassed, for God's sake, I'd gone up there as the daughter's boyfriend and I fell for the mother. I didn't know what to say to them. It would be an insult to the girl. So I came back to Bangkok with the girl and then went back on my own. At first, the mother didn't really want to know. She was really knocked out when she saw me come back alone. She thought I'd come with bad news, her daughter was dead or something. I had some difficulty explaining to her it was her I wanted. Don't ask me why. She was closer to my age; and when she was dressed up, she was a pretty attractive woman. Nothing really came of it. I went up there a couple of times, but *her life was there. She hadn't been in the sex trade. She had no idea of what her daughter was doing in Bangkok. When the daughter found out, she just laughed.*

Perhaps it is because a large proportion of men going to Bangkok are older that quite a number seem to have made relationships with women who were no longer young. Does this suggest a more realistic appraisal of their chances of making a relationship last? Some certainly said so.

Rafiq is in his late thirties. He works in the jewel trade. He is originally from Uttar Pradesh in northern India, but his family now lives in Bombay. He does not want them to join him in Thailand. His four children are all at school and he does not wish to interrupt their education. In any case, he says, his wife would not like Thailand. He found it very shocking when he first came here 12 years ago. Now he loves it and finds India repressive and narrow-minded.

I use the bars here. I like Thai women. I'm afraid that our Indian women, although they are beautiful, grow up without any knowledge of sex at all. When I first married, my wife was very ignorant. She had three brothers, but I think she had never seen a male sex organ. She was frightened and cried a great deal. She did not welcome sex with me. If this had not been the only way to make children, she would have avoided it. As it was, she never found pleasure in sex. Her fear also limited me. I didn't want to hurt her or to make her do anything against her will. It was very difficult.

I seized the opportunity to come to Bangkok. At first, I didn't know what excited me so much, apart from going abroad, seeing a kind of life that no one in India – except maybe the very rich – can know. Now I know that what it has done is to make me free. I have been liberated by Bangkok. I know what it is to take pleasure in the body of a woman, to enjoy sex. I shall always be thankful to the women in the bars for that. The first time, I was very frightened and I felt guilt. But the woman made it easy. It is as though they understand these things.

He shows me a photograph, which he carries everywhere, a smudgy picture of a woman in a saree and four smiling children.

I love my wife and children. I feel that as long as I am here and they stay there, I can keep my two lives apart. One day I will have to go back to Bombay. I do not know what I will do then. But my wife has no wish to have any sexual contact with me. We have always been like strangers sexually, although she is a dutiful mother and a good wife. I think India makes a problem out of sex and Thailand doesn't. I do not go to the bars often – maybe once every three or four weeks. I have one regular girl who likes Indians and does not complain if we smell of curry. I am devoted to her; but I would not wish to marry them, because I do not think they have the sense of responsibility that Indian women have. Her children are at home with their grandparents and she rarely sees them. She sends money to them, but does not see them. I do the same thing, but it is different for a man. A mother is a mother and children need her.

On one occasion, I was staying in Bangkok for a few days and I went to a hotel. In an adjacent room, there were three young Australians. One night, they came in, each with a girl on his arm. They occupied the same room and apparently, had a good night together. Next day, I met one of them in the restaurant. He was drinking a beer on his own, looking a little downcast. I asked him what happened to his friends. 'I don't know. I guess they've gone to the bars.' I asked him why he was not with them. He grimaced: 'Once is enough.' I said, 'It sounded like you had a good party last night.'

   He looked at me and said 'Not really.' I expressed some surprise. He did not respond for some time, but after we had talked for a while, he said, 'I only came to be with my mate. I'm gay. I love him. He isn't gay. He doesn't know how I feel. I guess that is the closest I'm going to get to him, doing it together. I couldn't tell him. But it's hard work, playing at being one of the boys, when it's the boys you want to be with.' Then he caught my eye and his whole demeanour changed abruptly. He grinned and said 'Just kidding.' I'm still not sure.

For many foreigners in Thailand, it is axiomatic that Thais are not 'hung up about sex'. This is often asserted as a favourable contrast to repressed Western attitudes. Unfortunately, it is far from being the simple truth it is sometimes claimed to be. One sad and dramatic incident occurred while I was in Bangkok which gave the lie to this over-simplification.

An Australian friend, Kieran, who is living with his (male) lover, met a young man in his early twenties in Lumpini Park. The Australian had an 'open' arrangement with his friend and invited the young man to stay in the apartment with him for two or three days. He was a village boy, working in a factory in Bangkok making steel rods for construction. It soon became clear that this was his first encounter with gay people. He had a low sense of self-worth, didn't like his dark skin, his looks. He had been unsure of his sexuality and the brief time with Kieran crystallised something he had not perhaps wanted to acknowledge. It came to him as a revelation and in the space of two or three days, this young man fell in love with my friend and became so attached to him that he would not leave.

Kieran pointed out that he had not been invited to stay under false pretences. The conditions were clear from the beginning. Kieran had told him that he was not interested in monogamous relationships and that he had no intention of leaving his present boyfriend – who is a security guard – for this new acquaintance. Kieran stressed, however, that they could be friends, that he would introduce him to other gay people. He would be welcome to stay in the apartment from time to time, but could not stay there indefinitely. He would have to leave on Sunday, go back to his room in south Bangkok and return to work.

The young man stayed. On Sunday, he sat down to write two letters. Late in the afternoon, Kieran went downstairs to say goodbye to his friend who was working nights. While they were gone, the young man climbed up to the roof of the building and threw himself into the street below. He was killed instantly. Kieran saw his body hurtle through the air. A crowd gathered. The police came. There was no question of foul play. Kieran was shaken and upset. His first instinct was to flee, to leave the flat, to get out of Bangkok. The police interviewed Kieran. The young man had left a note saying that he could not bear to live, but that it was not Kieran's fault. The police declared the incident closed.

4

THE SEX INDUSTRY:
ECONOMIC AND SOCIAL BASE

To discover something about the economic function of the
sex trade, I visited Chulalongkorn University, one of the
foremost educational establishments in Thailand. It is in the
heart of the city and close to Patpong; an extensive compound, with shady gardens and marble tables and benches
for study, cool secluded places, where the tranquillity of
study is disturbed only by langourous blossoms or leaves
falling from the trees.

I spoke first with Dr Voravidh Charoenloet in the Department of Economics; what he says is only made more shocking by his mild-mannered way of speaking.

*Levels of corruption distort the economy and this has led to
almost 60 per cent of the wealth now concentrated in the
hands of 20 per cent of the people. The degree of inequality
and the promise of wealth generate illusions of easy money;
and prostitution, like gambling, appears to some of the poorest as the quickest and most likely means of getting a share.*

*Of course prostitution in Thailand is ancient; but it used to
be called, ironically a 'profession'. It became industrialised at
the time of the Vietnam war; and this fed the rage for 'development' of the past 20 years. Prostitution has been modernised,
systematised. Trafficking is in the hands of the mafia, in collusion with police and politicians. You cannot touch them. Much
of the speculative building boom in Bangkok has been a means
of laundering black money, whether from prostitution, drugs or
illegal logging, which are three of the most lucrative trades in
the enterprise culture of Thailand.*

villages
due to sex tourist *less developed*

And indeed, if you go into some of the shopping malls – of which there are about 60 major developments in Bangkok – some of them are empty. There is simply no one around. They are ghostly places of glass and marble and expensive shops, with young women who sleep, head on their arms, resting on glass tables containing jewellery, silk or leather goods. The escalators move silently up and down without passengers; there are smart coffee bars and restaurants in which no one drinks or eats. It is highly disconcerting to those who are used to crowded shopping centres to find here this hushed, almost ecclesiastical, atmosphere.

Of course the condominiums make money. They are occupied; but their principal function is not to provide accommodation, but to make dirty money clean.

The costs of the Thai miracle are not counted. It is unfortunate that Thailand has the image of being at the centre of sex tourism; more so, since the costs of that, the spread of HIV, family breakdown, separations caused by migrant labour – anything betwen one and two million people migrate annually between Bangkok and the North and Northeast – are probably negative; but they do not show up as costs at all, because non-economic areas of life must absorb them.

It is the same with transport. There are rival interests fighting for a share of the money; and this immobilises the projects. The discussion about whether the Tananyong project for the Skytrain should go underground, the Hopewell Road and Rail project, the elevated road of the Expressway – all have been the focus of ceaseless debate and argument. This is because all politicians get some kickback from them. There have been endless questions about renegotiating them, changing the location or method of construction – if one political group can gain some advantage, they'll do it. But if Bangkok people mobilise to demand one form of transport rather than another, they'll say 'We have entered into contracts, we can do nothing about it.'

The previous government had said it would do something about corruption. Chuan Leek Pai (Prime Minister of Thailand until 1995) was of peasant origins, he had some understanding of popular concerns. But he was so tightly surrounded by business people, those who virtually took over the country after the withdrawal of the military, that he could do nothing. These now dominate the country in every way. The trouble is that wealth used to be considered a concept much wider, more ample than simply cash. The capitalist system needs to reduce all the different varieties of wealth in the world – the use value of things, the commons, the free things that are available, as well as free services and gifts between human beings – into money, because they can control and manipulate money and they can force the whole country to accept their measure of wealth; this is how they remain the controlling force in the land.

This is the context in which the sex industry operates. It is no good taking just one link in the chain, the most visible one, the relationship between sex workers and clients. Farangs who come here are haunted by the question 'Is it me she loves or my money?' Often, when they find out that she has a whole family depending on her, that is all they see and they assume this is proof of her bad faith. But she is a victim of the whole complex structure of the trade in flesh, of which the sexual encounter with the customer is only one element. It is all far more complicated than it appears.

One illustration. An American who came to live in Bangkok after the Vietnam war had a capital of around 150,000 dollars; at that time, it seemed reasonable that, with care, he might live off it for a foreseeable future. He had been wounded and could no longer work. He met a girl in a bar, who promised to look after him. Over time, he saw his modest wealth transferred, tangibly, into the house his girlfriend had built. This was to be his refuge. The family had a little land. He would live frugally, but would want for nothing. After a decade, his money had dwindled to almost nothing and he was sick. When it came to the pay-off, his girlfriend was off, nowhere to be found. He had no right to the house which belonged to her parents. Sick, damaged by alcohol, he went back, penniless, to the United States; embittered and angry. A transfer of resources had occurred on a very small scale; and the cheated man was outraged, although what had occurred was nothing compared to the vast removal of resources which travel from global poor to global rich, from south to north, and at which protests are muted. This is because the transfer in the latter case – some, notably Malaysian economist Martin Khor, estimate it as much as 500 billion US dollars a year – is conducted through terms of trade, financial institutions, debt and transfer pricing within the multinational companies, it is not cheating. 'This is economics', says Dr Charoenloet, and therefore, beyond contestation.

Dr Kua is a demographer at the University of Chulalongkorn; but he is no mere manipulator of figures. I spent a morning with him in September 1995 and discovered with delight that he has the rare gift of clothing his understanding of population movements and change with the breathing flesh and blood of human destinies: an enthralling moment.

The number of female workers who depend on the sex industry is fairly small. The official number is 70,000, but that is unreliable. It could be anything between 50,000 and 200,000. There are no fewer than 21 different kinds of commercial sex worker – from karaoke bars, to makers of videos, parlours with cubicles for sex upstairs, barbers, massage houses, beauty parlours for men and women, call girls, discos, beer bars, nightclubs, escort agencies, caddy-girls in golf clubs. There is a considerable range of activity.

The social costs are incalculable. The number who are HIV positive is now about 700,000. The rate of increase is, however, slower than it was. There is almost 100 per cent condom use in brothels now. Commercial sex workers have regular check-ups and the brothels can be closed if HIV infection is found. Because of campaigns conducted against the spread of HIV, disease among sex workers is in decline for the first time: cases of both syphilis and gonorrhoea are also decreasing. In fact, these things are becoming more and more confined to the less educated, low income groups, who remain relatively untouched by the mass media – those in labouring work, people who might drink and then go to a hotel or brothel. Of course, HIV is still growing: it is the rate of increase that has begun to register a decline.

For it to become more effective, the government has to concentrate on more education for the poor. That does not mean simply extending schooling – it is the quality of instruction that counts, not the lengthening of time in the formal system.

The government has not understood the importance of investing in people. Since the 1960s, economic growth has been the only objective. There has been no concern for public health. There has been no effort to help poor people understand why their children should go to school. They need the labour of their children because they are poor. Many of those who sell their children into prostitution are motivated, not by desire for gain, but by fear of perishing. There is a study of three villages in the North, where the researchers set out to discover who sold their children and why. It was the poorest who did so, the least educated. They saw their neighbours send their children to Bangkok and the only consequences they saw were that their neighbours then acquired new houses, goods for the household, television sets, videos, motorbikes.

The Ministry of Education has set up a project, not only to extend education, but also to give money to students and their families, so that they are not driven by the most basic urgency of survival. When children go to school for nine years, they can then continue vocational training, nursing school or whatever. Choice is the crucial element. It is no good preaching to those who have no alternative.

We are seeing some results of the intensive efforts to spread awareness of AIDS. In June 1994, the number of women attending ante-natal clinics in the whole kingdom who were found to be HIV-positive was 1.8 per cent. In the northern part of Thailand it reached 6.2 per cent. Six months later, December 1994, the figures had come down to 1.6 per cent for the kingdom and 5.1 per cent in the North.

Men from the Upper North have been coming to Bangkok or Pattaya, working as labourers, in factories, on construction sites. They go to the low-cost brothels, get infected and then, when they return home, they pass this on to their wives. This is a very dangerous process and, unless the poor are made aware of it, it can become very damaging to a whole generation of workers in Thailand.

Bangkok now has about 16 per cent of the population of Thailand; between 40 and 50 per cent are first-generation migrants; and about one-third of these are from Isan. Figures have to be interpreted. In Bangkok, there are 3.3 million people on the voters' lists, registered as having some livelihood here, 4.5 million people live in the city according to the census. But there are at least 1.8 million who are working and are not on the voters' list. Thirty per cent of the people working are migrants, daily migrants, as well as all those who still come and go seasonally to their home province. Some studies show that Bangkok has a population of 10 million by day and 7 million by night.

Fourteen hundred congested areas in the city containing 1.2 million people have been identified. That means one in six people are living in congested places, usually so that they can be close to their place of labour.

The shifting, drifting population can be seen by the springing up of so many 7–11 stores, which are open all night, Kentucky Fried Chicken restaurants which do not close, in order to serve people working shifts.

The 7–11 stores are always crowded, even at three o'clock in the morning. These convenience stores also serve those people who have a room or a space in a condominium in Bangkok for five days a week and then go home at weekends. I am one of them. I have a flat in a condo here and I migrate, if you like, with the whole family from Monday to Friday, although our home is in Nonthaburi. If I commuted on a daily basis and the children were at school here, we would be getting up every morning at 5.30. These are what economists call 'opportunity costs'. I buy 30 square metres of space in Bangkok for weekdays. I pay 40,000 baht a month interest. These are costs I bear. I am prepared to pay because I can. Most, of course, cannot and this is why the roads into the city are choked long before dawn, from 4.30 in the morning onwards.

It is a question of quality and equality. Most people do not have a choice in either education or health. Ten per cent of people die before they are 60. Of those surviving over 60, 20 per cent have some severe disability. Between 25 and 30 per cent of people over 60 lead impaired lives. So even if economic growth has given a greater life expectancy, people who live to be over 60 do not know how to live. It is something new. People never expected to live so long, so no preparations are made to enable people to live with disability, infirmity. If the quality of life is impaired, how are we better off? Longevity of itself is a pointless achievement.

Since people become richer, they live longer, they eat more and better food, but they become a social cost to their family or to society, because there has been no preparation for this.

However, studies of three-generation families show that 80 per cent of the elderly live with their children. Those over 60 are not seen here as a burden but as an asset: they provide essential childcare for their own children who have gone to the city to work. In Bangkok, less than 5 per cent of children attend nursery school: because of exorbitant land prices, nursery schools have sold their land for condominiums or malls. So when young people migrate to Bangkok, they leave their children with the grandparents; sometimes the parents see their own children only irregularly. The bond grows between young and old. Children in Thailand love old people; and this helps to strengthen family ties across the generations. Because between 60 and 70 per cent of people in Thailand are still farmers, they never retire; the three-generational pull remains a strong force for social cohesion. In this way, migration does not break but strengthens the family bond.

Eighty-two per cent of the elderly stay with one of their children. In the rural areas, the figure was 76 per cent in 1980 and 77 per cent in 1990. The question to ask is whether this is an index of greater exploitation or greater well-being? Is it because there is no alternative for the elderly or because there is a growing closeness between families? Do they stay together because this is the only security in a changing, shifting world?

The nuclear family actually decreased from 71 per cent in 1980 to 68 per cent in 1990. The extended family increased by one per cent from 25 to 26 per cent in the same period. If anything, we are seeing larger family units grow. The families are smaller, yes, but there is no evidence the bonds are breaking. In 1992, 96 per cent of the elderly were living with spouse, children or other relatives. Only 4 per cent live alone. In the US more than one-third of households consist of a single person.

Sex workers send their children to the village or leave them there with their grandparents. The children and the elderly survive on the earnings from the bars of Bangkok. It is very touching, very human; and it shows these rather garish places in a quite different light. In that sense, the sex industry is not a force for social disintegration. AIDS/HIV, that is another story. The cost of AIDS may eventually outweigh the income generated by sex tourism, indeed certainly will.

We should be finding more imaginative and sustainable ways of becoming prosperous; sooner or later, we shall all be impoverished by it. If 100,000 sex workers bring in 1000 US dollars each a year, that is a hundred million dollars a year – a very conservative estimate. But the social costs are being incurred in other places. They are just as real. There is a problem as long as we do not take account of the overall effect of our actions, but choose to see only what can be expressed in money terms. In this way, the arguments that occur abstractly in academic circles in the West have a starkness and a directness here, because it is all so much more visible. We can see the costs of our economic 'success' because they are etched upon the faces and the bodies of our people.

5

THE SEX INDUSTRY: SUPPLY

I

Commercial, international sex has flourished in Thailand since the 1960s, when the government contracted with the USA to provide rest and recreation services to troops in Vietnam. The entertainment sector made a significant contribution to the rapid industrialisation of the country in the 1970s. And even though a majority of the clients of prostitutes are Thai men, vested interests of the ruling elites made successive governments promote the expansion of tourism while integrating the sex industry with it. Between 1985 and 1990, earnings from tourism increased by 50 per cent, and it remains one of the country's major earners of foreign exchange. A *Bangkok Post* survey in 1987 found that almost 70 per cent of foreign tourists were single men.

Women's status in Thailand has been traditionally low. Until this century, men could legally give away or sell their wives and daughters. Double standards still prevail in attitudes to men and women. Thai society believes that boys are mischievous, men naturally promiscuous. Men need sex, but good women (this usually means the well-to-do) are expected to remain virgins until marriage. Prostitution is the only mechanism that can satisfy these asymmetrical arrangements – provide sex for men while enabling higher class women to remain virtuous. The ideology that traditionally subordinates female to male sexuality shifts as the people move to the cities. It migrates to the institutions of urban society: in the sex trade, the power of the bar owners, pimps, doctors, customers, replicates the power formerly residing with Buddhist institutions, the Thai military and the monarchy. Indeed, the monastery, military and monarchy had degraded the social and cultural position of women to such a degree that it was easy for the market to do the rest.

The women in the sex industry often regard themselves as small entrepreneurs. They believe that prostitution offers them a chance for upward mobility, the opportunity to meet a farang, to be kept by or marry a rich man, which will raise their status. Although this can happen, it is rather rare. Some women certainly end their working life better off than when they started, but they have rarely acquired alternative or transferable skills. Life after the sex trade usually depends on the acquisition of a little capital with which they can start some small business.

II

Buddhism values the non-self, non-attachment to the things of the world. In this context, women have been traditionally seen as activators of desire and were therefore despised and feared by the monks. Women were felt to be impure and carnal. The sexual misconduct of women is a consequence of their karma, their demerit in a former life. In this way, men can express lust without demerit because it is caused by women. Women must be reborn as men to achieve a high status. Even prostitutes, however, can still make merit if they save their families from poverty or donate money to Buddhist temples. At the same time (as also in Christianity), women are also inherently good because of their mothering and nurturing role.

If women enhance the well-being of the family they make merit. The image of the woman as breadwinner is common among sex workers. The idea of nurturer, in combination with poverty, has been exploited by the Thai government, tourist agencies, the media, to justify female migration and the sex industry; a deformation of care-giving. It is this particular quality which many foreign clients claim to value in Thai sex workers. 'They give that bit extra, they are considerate, they can't do enough for a man, they make you feel good' – all the familiar clichés are well grounded in material reality, although the significance of that reality usually remains concealed from their customers.

The influence of the military remains, although it is less powerful than business now in Thai society. The military

gained its power during the Ayutthaya period (1351–1767)
when kings strengthened the army to fight the Burmese. In
the late fifteenth/early sixteenth century, military service was
compulsory. Women were excluded from the military until
1985. The absorption of male labour into armies and into
corvee labour depleted the male workforce in the villages and
forced more women to support families; women were
strengthened within the household, but had little place in
the wider social institutions.

Women were also commodified by the military – accumulation of women and wives was a source of military prowess,
social prestige and wealth. Women were given as rewards for
military achievement in the Ayutthaya period. Female sexuality as a source of male pleasure and wealth was apparent in
the deep involvement of the military in the development of
the entertainment sector in the 1960s and 1970s.

Although monarchical power has decreased in the field of
social policy, historically, the kings had absolute control over
their subjects. In the Ayutthaya period, the Sakdina system,
which linked social rank to the allocation of land, was introduced. Rigid social stratification occurred, with the highest
status confined to a small ruling group, followed by monks
and novices, with serfs and slaves at the bottom. Corvee was
required of all males in the serf class for six months a year.
Slavery lasted until 1905. This left women to subsistence
labour. They were also forced into an indentured polygamy
and prostitution. In Brahminical culture, women of the ruling class were exchanged for pledges of loyalty between ruling
families and in answer to requests for military and political
protection. In the Court, women's role was decorative;
women of lower ranks were exchanged or taken as concu-
bines by elite men. Under the Sakdina system, women were
also taken to service Thai peasant men working on (compulsory) corvee labour for the nobility.

Prostitution developed in the nineteenth century with the
expansion of the rice export economy and the influx of male
Chinese migrants to the cities. The monarchical and aristo-
cratic ideology of male supremacy and promiscuity spread
downwards to the new urban population. Although monogamy
is the only legal form of marriage now, some Thai men still
register marriages to different women. There is no penalty for

polygamy. These values reached the people via schools, community, religious rituals, propaganda and the media.

The (present) Chakri dynasty restructured the Thai kingdom from the end of the eighteenth century, with the capital in Bangkok. Rama I tried to restore the glories of Ayutthaya and to revive the traditional ways of life in the new context, consolidating many of the Ayutthaya laws, including polygamy and the classification of wives. There were three orders of wife: (1) the principal, (2) the secondary and (3) the slave. Parental consent was required to take a principal wife. A secondary wife required the consent of the man. The slave wife was acquired through purchase and indebtedness. The categorisation was based on the law of 1361 which allowed men to punish wives more harshly. They could sell them and punish them corporally.

In the early nineteenth century, the pressure to open up to Western trade and communication left Thailand no longer unaware of Western criticism of slavery, polygamy and prostitution. Rama V and Rama VI had a Western education and sought to liberalise Thai society. In 1905 slavery was abolished by Rama V. Rama VI advocated monogamy and compulsory education for all Thais, including women.

The end of absolute monarchy came in 1932. Monogamy became the norm in 1935. Equal rights were granted in 1974. The status of women improved markedly under the new Constitution of 1974, but close examination reveals that the ruling class was reluctant to liberalise women's status completely. For instance, Sections 1445 and 1446 entitled a man to claim compensation from other men who had had sexual intercourse with a woman betrothed to him. Section 1516 allowed men to divorce on the grounds of a wife's adultery, while a wife 'must prove that her husband has maintained or treated another woman as his wife'. There is no legal sanction against bigamy. The tradition of 'minor wives' continues, but without being formalised.

After the abolition of slavery in 1905, many freed slave wives became prostitutes. To become 'free' with no land or means of subsistence naturally led to women being absorbed by brothels. The 1908 Contagious Disease Prevention Act sought to control places of prostitution, to limit the health effects of prostitution, not to make it illegal. This Act was abolished in 1960 when the Prostitution Suppression Act was passed. This made prostitution illegal and it is still in force. Prostitution is defined as 'an act of promiscuity rendering sexual services for remuneration'. Under this Act, prostitutes and pimps are subject to penalties, but customers are not. Penalties are relatively light – three months in prison, or a maximum fine of 1000 baht.

The Entertainment Places Act of 1966 further legitimised prostitution indirectly. This Act was designed to control the operations of places of entertainment which endanger public order or morals. Women are expected to provide only 'special services', which are open to the customer's request. Thus the operators of the sex industry are protected by an unclear definition of 'special services'. This also contributes to the unequal relationships between employers and workers, because the latter are exposed to legal sanctions, while the former are free to operate as they please. The law normalises the traditional subordination of women and commodification of their sexuality.

III

In order to find out something about the options available to women in the sex industry, I met Thanavadee Thajen, of the Friends of Women Foundation, in Bangkok. The Friends of Women Foundation is an NGO, with an office and shop at Payathai, off Paholyathin, away from the tourist areas. It provides legal services for women, in the sex industry, in marriage and divorce and campaigns for alternatives to prostitution.

We have networks all over the country, trying to find not only other forms of employment, but also outlets for the crafts and skills of women. It is vital that they receive an adequate reward for their work in the village or locality where they live. We promote handicrafts – sewing, making bamboo and grass baskets, ornaments and traditional jewellery, tie-dyeing – so that they have choices other than coming to Bangkok or other tourist resorts and drifting into the sex industry.

In this part of the city, there are few foreigners and no sex tourism. But sex parlours for local men, brothels and bars are everywhere. Sometimes these have a front as a restaurant, beauty salon or hairdresser, anything that does not attract official attention. The fact that they are not open brothels makes it more difficult to reach those working there. Many women are virtual prisoners. Some never go out. The establishments are sometimes controlled by powerful mafia groups, business people with links to politicians and the police. These are more oppressive to women than the open international sex industry, because there, at least, there is some transparency and openness and the women can come and go as they choose.

There has been an active trade in girls from Burma and Laos. Sometimes they are kidnapped and brought to Bangkok. In Thailand also, in some of the villages where we go, parents bring a photograph to us and say 'Have you seen our daughter? She disappeared 18 months ago.'

We also provide legal advice to women who want to leave prostitution, who want to go home, or who want to get away from a violent man. Sometimes a Thai man may have two or three wives. It is the men who are the problem. Men have always used prostitutes, only it has now become more of a business, more ruthless too. Prostitution has become an industry rather than a service, more competitive. Consumerism only gives a new twist to the idea that men's desires must not be thwarted, even if that means prostitution, rape, violence to women. These things may have deep cultural roots, but they receive a powerful new stimulus from 'modernisation', international tourism and so on. This is why it is not easy to speak of 'eradicating' the sex industry, because it has evolved out of our own history.

We often ask why Westerners come to Bangkok. What are they looking for and why do they think they can find it here and not in their own country? The problem must be tackled at the point of demand, both with Thais and foreigners. The easy – and traditional – way out is to blame the women.

The Friends of Women Foundation was set up 15 years ago, when the then Japanese Prime Minister visited Thailand. We went to him to protest at the numbers of Japanese tourists coming here to use Thai women; and from there, the work took off. We see many examples of the brutality with which women are treated. In Phuket, there was a fire in a brothel in which five women were burned to death *because they were locked into the building. There have also been many cases where women ran away from brothels and complained to the police of having been kept there against their will, but nothing happened to their captors. One woman took cyanide in a police station because she was so desperate and no one would listen to her. These stories are just the tip of the iceberg: women are threatened, even disfigured, or shot, if they attempt to leave.*

Of course there are places where the women work openly and can leave if they want to. The worst abuses occur in those brothels where the women have been bought as a commodity. The needs of women do not enter into the calculation. It is the service of male desire that still dominates their function in Thailand and they can be cruelly ill-used, either in serving those interests, or equally, if they try to resist them. Some women become emancipated, aware and proud and we also see many of them. But they tend to leave the industry, get educated and take other work. We have 30 women in Beijing this week. [This was at the time of the United Nations Conference on Women in September 1995.]

In the local brothels, the health checks which are supposed to take place monthly are rarely carried out. If a woman is found to be HIV-positive, she must leave. In places where the traffic in women ensures a constant supply of new young girls, why should they care? HIV is now being taken seriously by the government, because the men who have migrated to Bangkok are increasingly taking it back into the rural areas. It is spreading that way and may well become a major crisis for Thailand. When it hits men, that is when it becomes a social issue. Until that time, it remains a women's issue; which is the same thing as saying it is of lesser importance.

We are also going into the universities with programmes to try to change the behaviour of the next generation. Even educated young men do not think it is good to control their desires; and the context in which we are working only makes that worse. 'Liberalisation' is a fashionable word; and it spreads into areas other than the economy, where its effects can be disastrous. There is much hypocrisy in this. The consumer society is about the infinity of desires: in the peeling away of all the repressions, some strange desires are bound to emerge. To deny these any outlet is hypocritical,

*when so many other disordered, dehumanising behaviours
are not only sanctioned, but are regarded as essential for the
growth of the economy. We do not see our own distortions
because we are accustomed to them. Only when we see
pederasts and other horrors, we see ourselves mirrored at our
worst and we do not like what we see.*

Beth is an American working with EMPOWER, where she
teaches English to women in the bars of Patpong. The idea
is to enable women to deal with customers on a more equal
basis. The Centre is in Patpong itself, surrounded by the
stalls of vendors of T-shirts, fake Rolex watches, Thai silk
scarves, jewellery and porn magazines; all around, the bars
have their daytime somnolence, dingy faded photographs of
girls in glass cases, neon lights diminished by sunshine, the
interiors of chipped wood and garish paint that will be
drowned in vivid light after dark. The Centre is in a building
owned by the King's Group, one of the bigger and more
responsible companies in the sex trade, which owns 15 bars.

The office of EMPOWER here is next to a beauty parlour,
a large functional space, where women are having mani-
cures, pedicures, hairstyling and dyeing, facelifts and skin
treatments, removal of moles and blemishes. They sit on
leatherette benches with high wooden backs, a bit like the
Outpatients department of a hospital, waiting their turn for
the treatment in front of big tarnished mirrors that will
make them even more perfect, more irresistible, more likely
to attract the punters. As I go in in the early evening, two
young women are coming out of the clinic run by the
company which owns the bars. They are holding pieces of
cotton wool against the vein in their upper arm, waiting
for the bleeding to stop after a blood test. Their chunky
shoes echo on the stone steps as they clatter out into the
daylight, their laughter echoing in the cavernous stairwell
of the building.

The Centre is also a quiet place where women receive
counselling or share problems informally. EMPOWER is also
running a government scheme to help them catch up on lost
educational opportunities. Some of the women are highly
motivated; and many are extremely competent. Some have
already acquired bar English, functional and direct.

The problem for most women is the lack of power, their unwillingness, or powerlessness, to resist exploitation. The discipline is very rigorous for the women. The foreigners who come and fall in love with them, they deserve everything they get. These women are working and working damned hard. They might start on a monthly salary of 3000 baht, but deductions, a system of fines – for coming late to work, for failing to get enough customers, for not reaching their quota in getting customers to buy drinks from the bar – means that their salary may be reduced to near zero. If one makes a date with a punter bypassing the bar and the other workers see her, they'll tell and that's another offence for which she can be fined – it is a fiercely competitive business.

Some of the women can earn, but on average they are not making big money. A few who are lesbian maybe work with greater detachment. A few of the toms work on the doors as touts and hustlers getting the customers in. Most establishments do not have rooms for sex on the premises. The punters pay the bar and take the girls off to hotels. 500 baht would be considered enough by most of the girls, 1000 is still really quite something. But Westerners who come and think they've found love, Jesus, they should see the conditions the women live and work in! The behind-the-scenes of the bars are often squalid, crowded and dirty. They live in poor places, in shared rooms in hot airless buildings with inadequate bathing facilities and toilets. There is often a whole family depending on them and that may include brothers as well as parents, younger sisters and brothers. I'm always surprised how many say they have adult brothers who do nothing and expect to be kept by them. Quite a lot also have children.

Although in many ways Thai society is cruel, Western society is hard and cruel in a different way. The West denies tenderness to the old, the ugly, the defeated. They come here and think they have found it. But basically, they are paying for an illusion. If you take a young woman to some upmarket hotel, she sees some high life, she may have a good time. But she'd rather have the money. It isn't long before the farang gets disappointed; that's when they start coming out with all this stuff 'You never know what they're thinking', 'They string you along', 'I thought I had a relationship with a girl and I found I'd got 42 relations to keep as well.'

Their bodies are the only social security their families have. It is difficult for a Westerner to understand what a solemn, awesome thing that is. Not that we should sentimentalise the Thai family – some parents sell their daughters, for God's sake.

The owners of the bars try to make it even more competitive – they set the women against one another, because the last thing they want is any kind of solidarity or revolt. And they don't get it. There may be affection and friendship among the women, but it remains an individualistic business with no sentimentality where the punters are concerned. A woman knows when she gets too old – every day is a kind of popularity poll, the minute she starts to slip, she knows it. Some become Mama Sans, others go to work for cleaning companies or serve in bars.

Thai culture is seductive, but it's a superficial seductiveness. What you don't see in the bars is the hidden violence that drives young women from the village to Bangkok, Chiang Mai, Hat Yai and into the industry. I don't know the statistics and I'm not sure it helps. I only know it exists on a big scale. Of course, all countries have a big sex industry, especially where there are many migrant male workers. Delhi and Dhaka both have a big sex trade, but foreigners don't go there. This is why Thailand concerns and fascinates the West, because of the high profile it has and the sheer numbers of men who come here.

The growing assertiveness of Western women is also a factor which sends men here. Women here know how to behave in a submissive way, that is, they know how to be sexist for the men. You hear a lot of men say this is why they like them. 'They're real women': the implication being that the men who say it are real men and that Western women have become defeminised.

Prostitutes are despised, although 90 per cent of Thai men use them. There are not the levels of hate that you find in the West. It is rare to find crimes of random violence against women, although violence certainly occurs in interpersonal relationships. But the idea of serial killers stalking women because they are prostitutes is, I think, quite unknown here.

There are several kinds of sex tourists. Some come for an

orgiastic few days. Some come regularly to see a particular woman they've established a relationship with. Others are hooked on sex or on the search for love, something exotic, who knows.

Also, what you do to foreign women is different, it doesn't count. Racism is an integral part of sex tourism. About two-thirds of visitors to Thailand are lone males; out of six million a year, that is a lot of men. Not all are sex tourists, but it keeps the trade buoyant. The young men who come in groups are increasingly European white trash, a know-nothing macho culture out for a good time, which they are going to get whatever it costs. Others are more serious, looking for relationships. They can be even more dangerous, because they get involved and if they are disappointed they can be violent. I don't say it doesn't happen – there are marriages, friendships that last for years.

Sex mostly is kept out of the bars. In some of the darker ones and the more basic places, they'll do a hand job or a blow job, but mostly the clients have to take the girls off. The men flatter themselves that they're showing the women a good time, but in fact, they've all been to those places times without number, the smart restaurants and five star hotels.

The industry isn't static. There is a high turnover. There are women who stay for years, but generally, they come and go. A woman might spend a few months, a year, with one guy and be out of circulation for that time. The number at any one moment is not high. A couple of streets in Patpong, it isn't much. But with all those who have been in and out of it, it adds up. But for every woman who has been in the business, there will be 95 who are working in garment factories, industrial units, hotels and department stores. You have to keep it in proportion.

IV

One evening I went back to the EMPOWER office to talk with some of the women studying there: they undermine all the stereotypes. For one thing, many of those who come here have considerable insight into the relationships between themselves and the foreigners. They are also very ordinary: working women, with a lively humour and sense of irony. Many come from rural areas and, when they are not at

work, they are not particularly glamorous. Many are thoughtful and more serious than their reputation.

The women are disadvantaged by the nature of their
work, the terms of their employment, the conditions in
which they labour. The efforts of EMPOWER are not simply to
teach them to deal more effectively with customers and bar
owners, although that is the ostensible purpose of the classes
they attend; the wider objective is to build confidence among
those whose self-esteem has been damaged, who feel shame
and guilt and have not repaid their family what they feel
they owe them. They can rarely stand up for themselves at
work because of the unanswerable logic of the market – if
they don't like it, they can make way for those who will.

Beth says: 'A man will come in, prepared to spend 1000
baht. By the time he has paid for a drink and the off-fee to
the bar, he will only have 200 baht to offer to the woman.
In the past, she had no option but to accept. At least when
she has learned to speak English she can explain to the
customer what is expected of him, what the hidden costs of
his night out will be. She can negotiate a better deal for
herself. These are small gains, but significant. They increase
her control over her working environment.'

The women are emphatic that they do not want to be
seen as victims. They know their stories are sad, even
harrowing. But they are dignified, capable and, although vulnerable, they are neither passive nor helpless. What does not
appear in a brief statement of their situation are the sometimes heroic efforts to achieve what look like small changes
in their lives; the endurance and stoicism with which they
have managed oppression, violence and poverty. 'It is a complex and ambiguous story, being a sex worker. They have
little power in relation to the bar owners and employers, yet
with customers they display great inventiveness and ingenu-
ity and they use these qualities to enhance their income.'

Early on a Monday evening; the dead evening of the week.
In the EMPOWER building there are two classes in the same
room, about 18 women, siting on metal chairs around plastic
tables. When the classes finish at 5.30, some of the young
women stay behind to reflect on their life and experience.

Nan, in her early twenties, is five months pregnant. She
has now stopped bar work. Her Australian boyfriend, who is

working for a computer company in Bangkok and whose baby she is carrying, has taken her into his flat. They have lived together for one year. She says he has a wife in Australia. He tells Nan he will get divorced. I ask if his wife know about her. Nan is not sure. She speaks in metaphors. 'You cannot trust anyone 100 per cent. The only one you can trust is yourself. And if you believe in yourself, other people may. I cannot be with him, nor can he be with me, every minute of the day. That would be boring, horrible. I have to have my own life and he must have his. I don't know what he is doing. I believe he loves me because I believe I love him. But you can never be sure. You cannot be sure of your feelings tomorrow or next week.'

Nan already has one child, who is at home with her parents in Ayutthaya. She expresses the caution of many of the women who have been in and out of the sex industry for many years; 'rescued' by a farang, or a Thai, for six months, a year, two years, sometimes married, sometimes not. When the relationship fails, they return to work in the bars. A kind of melancholy fatalism lies beneath the smiles: you cannot make long-term plans, you cannot answer for your feelings or anyone else's, you do not how you will be treated by the next farang. All that is solid is the indissoluble bonds of family and the village roots; but to return there without money is impossible.

'You hope it will last. At first you expect it', says Noy, who is 27. 'But every time it breaks down, you are disappointed and next time, you expect a bit less of it. So as time goes by, it has to be better in order to survive as long as the previous one. Men will make promises to a woman. That is their nature. We have to learn not to believe in them too much.'

Tip, who is 24, has not been working in the bars for some months either. She is living with a Britisher. She is an animated, self-aware woman, who expresses herself easily in a haphazard though expressive English. She is living in a temporary happy-ever-after: that curiously provisional permanence that seems to characterise so many relationships with farangs. They know it is temporary but they have to suspend disbelief: you can't live your life as though everything is doomed. So when things go well, you live in a state of euphoria.

At such times the tensions are very obvious between those who have a boyfriend and the women who have no such relationship and must still work each day in the bars. On the other hand, if a relationship goes on for too long, becomes stale, the women become bored and admit a longing to return to the excitement and the perpetual unknown of the bars. 'Sometimes, you know he just wants to come in and watch television and eat and go to sleep. If you've done nothing all day but some shopping or meeting a friend for an ice-cream, you hate those long evenings doing nothing. And you look at your watch and you think "Oh everything will just be starting now in the bar" and he is getting ready for bed.'

Nok is a more mature woman; she wears her long hair loose and in class she is wearing a smart red and black dress – the kind of thing you might expect to see in the bar. Nok is unusual in that she did not enter the industry until she was 30. She separated from her first husband, and her two children remain with his parents. Her second husband died when Nok was just 30; and for her, this was the only way to make a living. She is perhaps 34 or 35, extremely handsome and giving the lie to those who say the life of sex workers is finished at 30. Nok is a passionate woman, whose convictions are at odds with the easy-going Tip. Nok says she is always looking for a relationship with the farang in the bar. No, she doesn't mind if the men are old or unattractive or ill-mannered. The worse they are, the higher she will charge. It is common for the more attractive women to pass on the men they don't like to workers who are less choosy.

'While you are working it is better not to have a regular boyfriend', says Nan. 'But you work to get money and a relationship; but if you love money more than a relationship, you can forget marriage or security. There has to be a balance. Greed can work against you. Do not ask for too much, or he will think that you do not care for him.'

It was an irony that the perceptions of the women by the foreign men – some of which I had earlier discussed with the women – were more or less reflected in the view which the women have of the men. 'They promise everything, but give you as little as possible.' 'They say they are looking for love or affection, but all they want is sex. Afterwards, they are not interested.' 'The men say they want love, but really want sex', say the women; 'The women say they want love but really want money', say the men.

Tip came from near Pattaya when she was 14 to find work that would help her support her poor family. She came to Bangkok with a friend, knowing quite clearly what she would do. And she is proud to have built a new house for her parents, to have recycled the wealth of countless farangs into concrete and bricks which, to her, represent security, solid and tangible, the more impressive because it has been salvaged out of something so fleeting and evanescent as male desire. They have created something out of nothing, the material proof that they are dutiful daughters; like women in a fairy tale who spin the straw of lust into pure gold. This is where they feel they exercise their real power, even though that power remains in the service of gratitude to fathers and mothers, working off the indissoluble bondage of duty to kindred; which, in some measure, is the last repository for the old, feudal patriarchal values. Tip was herself a child prostitute. She is lively, intelligent and apparently well-balanced young woman. This does not retrospectively make it all right that she had to find a living in this way. Many sex tourists who seek out children like to hear that 'girls grow up faster in the Third World', that they have been 'on the game' for years before, so that the punter does not appear to be responsible for her fate.

Nit also came into the industry at the late age of 27, after the break-up of a relationship. Nit is from Bangkok and has three children. Her boyfriend was Thai but when they split up, she went back to live with her mother and brother. Two of the children are with the mother of the boyfriend, the other is in Chiang Mai with her married sister. In spite of the fragmenting and scattering of families, the bonds remain. The strong sense of duty is not diminished by all the uprootings and separations. Nit works at the Pussy Galore bar: the nighttime working person could not be more different from matter-of-fact daily life. On stage, there are multicoloured lights, revolving crystal balls, the catwalks and chromium poles, the deafening sound system. 'There, we are objects of desire. There, all is confusion. Here, we are trying to make sense of our lives.'

No, they say, it does not demean them, showing themselves to foreigners in the bars. Their being is separate from their body. In one sense they cannot be reached by the hands of those who purchase their services. Nit says that the women form clusters of friends who protect and look after each other, even though the competition for customers in the bar can be fierce. 'Some girl will come and break into your conversation, especially if she can speak French or Japanese or whatever it is better than you can. Some women do quarrel, but on the whole, when we are working, we are friendly.'

The go-go dancers earn a basic salary of 3000–5000 a month. It depends on their physical beauty. There is a clear and rigid hierarchy in the market value of individuals; everyone knows where she stands and those lower in the scale yield to those who can command more. If the women do not dance, their basic salary is 2500–2800 a month (a little over 100 US dollars).

'We have to go with a customer a minimum of once a week. There is a bonus for every time we go with another, 100 baht a time [4 US dollars]. We used to have to sell a certain number of drinks every night, but some bars have stopped that now. If you go with someone more than six times, you get an extra 200 baht a time.' These precarious bonuses are easily offset by the system of fines and losses. A woman who fails to come to work on a minimum of 26 days out of 28 loses 200 baht for a weekday, 500 if she doesn't show on a Friday, Saturday or Sunday.

Tip says she has frequently been with 14 or 15 a month. There are regular and compulsory health checks. If they are found to be ill, the girls themselves must pay for medicine, antibiotics. If a woman is HIV-positive, she is out. 'We are fined for being late', says Nok. 'There is no freedom. Our pay is cut at any excuse. This is why there is such pressure for girls to find a boyfriend or a farang who will take them out of it, at least for a time. But they cannot get from one man all the money they need unless he is a tycoon; so emotional security is often paid for with loss of income. Many women move between the two, alternately working and living with a farang.'

Most of the women have done other work. They do not become sex workers because it is easy. To confront farangs, sometimes drunk, often old, not infrequently dirty, every day with a serene smile and the pretence that he is what you have been waiting for all your life is a constant violence against them. Nit used to sell food outside the house where they live, soup and noodles, homely fare in plastic bags. She says her only other skill is sewing, but she didn't want to go into a garment factory. The alternative was to try her luck in Patpong. She came with a friend and found work immediately.

Tip says you are never too old. In one bar where she worked, there was a woman in her fifties. She doesn't get many men; but some men are clever and, by choosing a woman who is older, they have more chance of making it last. Some of the women also deliberately set out to find an old man, because there is more chance that old men will be faithful and will leave them some money when they die. Nan says that sometimes men in their seventies just want to talk, will give 500 baht just for a few minutes' chat and 500 baht if you talk to them for an hour. 'They want company, not sex. That is also part of the job.'

Nok says the men come to find happiness. 'A woman will say "I love you" to all the men. It might not be true; you say it because it is part of your working dialogue, part of the ritual. And sometimes the men might believe it and pay more; and sometimes it might even become true. She says "I love you" because she needs the money. She's not going to say "I don't love you" or "I hate you", although these might also be true. You say it in English, because in English it doesn't count. You don't say *Chan ra kun*, because for us, the Thai words are special.'

Tip says: 'I like it when the men say "You come shopping with me", men who just want to enjoy. They might have a family and want a woman for fun. Then your job is to have fun. If he wants love, then you have to give him love.'

Nok says: 'When you first see a man, if you don't like the look of him, you wait to see what he offers and if it's enough, you overcome your dislike. The first question I always ask myself is "Can I trust him?" and before I'll go any further the answer has to be yes. When I look at a customer, I see what he looks like and then if he's passable, the next thought is "Could I have a relationship with him, could I like him?" And if that is not possible, I won't go with him.'

Nan does not ask about money if she sees someone

whose girlfriend she would like to be. Tip says most women do not think that way. But her experience is different; having come here at 14 to survive, she judges the situation very clearly. 'I don't go free with anyone. I always ask about money, but I always think relationship as well. You wonder how much you can get out of him. Perhaps he will take care of you, buy you a car, anything. When I first started, I was very scared. I wouldn't want it to happen to anyone else. The first man in the bar said "She's not very sexy, she's too young." I was angry, I kicked him. But after the first time, it gets easier. I stopped working at 17 to live with my boyfriend. Then when he dropped me, I went back to work again. I stayed with one farang, but I was bored. Doing nothing. In an apartment. Just waiting for him to come in. He told me to go back to work in the end and I was pleased.'

Nit makes men pay more money if they are ugly, not attractive or, more importantly, not polite.

Tip does not send money home now; her sister, who is also in Bangkok, sends money home. She bought a car although she could not drive. She had a Thai boyfriend who left her to go to Germany and now she is taking care of her British boyfriend. She has given him the car she had bought. When she first started sex work, she took pills and drank so that she would not care. She had more confidence when she was on drugs. Now that she is in a relationship, this is no longer necessary.

Nok says she can take care of herself; she does not send money to the parents of the children's father in Khonkang in the Northeast. She feels sad about what has happened in the past, but she hopes the future will be better. If you have a boyfriend, you fear he might die. 'Sometimes I feel it is better not to have anyone; but then I think who will take care of me when I am old?' I ventured to say that is what you have children for. 'Yes, but how do you know in the future whether a baby will take care of you? You can't have children just to take care of you.'

Tip asks: 'How could I raise a child? I already have one in Ayutthaya and I'm here.'

Of the five women, three said they believe there is more suffering than happiness in their life; the others said it was equal. There is a preoccupation with having someone to look after you, whether it be a husband, a boyfriend, a child, a relative. Since there is no other form of welfare, there is no other source of security. 'What will happen to me?' is a constant question. Nan said that if she had a choice, she would not be doing this work. Tip would work 'in an office' if she could choose, in an air-conditioned room. Nok would be a housewife and so would Nit; she would let her children study. Nan has already worked in a fish-canning factory. Being a sex worker is far preferable to that.

The women do not see themselves as victims. They agree there is an element of choice – after all, most women who come to Bangkok do not enter the sex industry. Far more are working in factories and in garment manufacture. They work in the bars primarily for security, especially for their families; yet paradoxically, it is one of the most insecure of jobs, with a fairly brief working life, which is susceptible to illness, especially now in the age of AIDS. It is, they say, wonderful to be admired, to be desirable; but it is also competitive and ruthless. They oscillate between working and intervals of luxury with longer-term boyfriends, a cycle of stability and uncertainty. In the end, it is also addictive; fraught with potential for what *might* happen if you meet the right man at the right time. 'It is a gamble'; and indeed, many of the women do gamble, at cards or mah-jong. You have to be a certain kind of personality to do the work successfully. The women are intelligent, dignified; yet always hopeful, always vigilant, on the lookout for deliverance from something they cannot easily break away from. The dream of security is better, said Tip, if it remains a dream; the reality is boring, makes you impatient to be back in the bar, with the women, the excitement, the promise of a new encounter.

I met Chi in a fast food restaurant; the daughter of a Thai father and Chinese mother. She is 28, working in a bar, but also studying English so that she can become a tourist guide. She is a reflective and slightly melancholy young woman, brought up by her grandfather and fascinated by her family's history. Her grandfather came with his brother from China. Their parents had died and they were forced to live on roots of tarow; they worked on a ship coming to Thailand, a journey of one month in 1916. When they arrived in Bangkok, he worked emptying the spittoons in the bars of the neighbourhood where they settled. He married and had ten children. 'They are all scattered now', says Chi, 'and I am the only one left who stays with my grandfather.' The grandfather eventually owned a lard shop and Chi helped as a child; but with the change in eating patterns in the country, as diet became more diverse, she could see no future in it.

She is now learning the language of tourism by day in a private university and dancing in long white boots and a silver lurex dress by night. Chi says she is two different people, yet neither of them is her real self. She is reading an English language book and is learning a sentence that describes the carvings in a temple: 'The mouldings represent the Buddhist cosmology – primordial instincts, the physical earthly existence and the sublimest thoughts.' She shows it to me, sighs and frowns. She is committing it to memory by rote. She asks me, 'What is cosmology?'

Her parents separated when she was five. Her mother now has two children, her father five, with other partners. She felt rejected by both of them. Without her grandfather, she would not have survived. She went to work at 16 in a bar that was only a few hundred metres from where she was living. Her grandfather knew nothing about it, but assumed she was working in a restaurant to provide for her studies. She says: 'I do not know why no one ever recognised me there. Perhaps he knew. He is very intelligent.'

They live in a wooden house, overshadowed by the new developments of Bangkok. It was built by Chi's grandfather on what was waste ground 'before Bangkok became developed'. In the house there is also one aunt, with her daughter, the same age as Chi. The aunt, says Chi, is 'a little crazy, because she has been without a partner for 25 years'. Chi says 'I do not wish to be like that.' She is devoted to her grandfather who is now well into his eighties. She has no objection to older men in the bars; they are more considerate and thoughtful. It is the young ones she avoids, because they are too selfish and insensitive. 'They can never remember my name. The old men, they always remember.'

There is an important cultural distinction to be made between the response of Thai women sex workers and sex workers in other (especially Western or Western-dominated) cultures. One element with Thais is that a large part of their being is not involved when they are working. I had written earlier: 'Their core remains untouched: their spirit is not engaged.' Julia O'Connell-Davison, who has extensively researched sex tourism and sex workers (see *Race and Class*, July 1996), objected that the kind of distancing which I had attributed to Thai women is very common among all sex workers; that they shut off their emotions, simply split life from livelihood, and that the outcome of this is nearly always psychologically damaging. She pointed out that even in Thailand, women sex workers do not go back to their families and quietly announce what they are doing. They describe themselves to their parents as 'waitresses' or 'receptionists'; which doesn't imply that sex work is as socially acceptable as many sex tourists would like to believe. I'm sure this is true; but it may also be that in cultures where sex is perceived as less problematical than it is in the West, the damage to the individual may be more limited. This is an area which could be usefully researched: are alleged 'cultural' differences merely a refined form of special pleading, or is the insistence that all women in sex work are damaged by it yet another piece of Western projection upon cultures they do not understand? This, like many aspects of cross-cultural emotional and sexual relationships, is in need of clarification.

V

Loy is 31. She works in a Patpong bar; she is small, with close-cut hair, wearing a yellow coat nipped in tightly at the waist and a short cream skirt. She wears a paper flower in her hair. I met her in the bar, told her what I was doing and invited her for a meal. She was nonplussed. I didn't want her to think that this was just another more subtle farang trick to get something for nothing. I told her I was gay. She went to ask her friends what they thought. I was immediately surrounded by about six young women who looked at me curiously, as though to decide whether I could be trusted or not. In the end, the consensus was that it was all right. Loy wouldn't go to a restaurant; she preferred one of the stalls in the street. We sat on Rama IV, a busy main road. Every time the traffic lights changed, a phalanx of motorbikes raced ahead of the four-wheelers in a crashing climax of noise and a swirl of bluish exhaust-smoke. This made conversation impossible and made the eyes sting. We ate prawns, noodles and soup, sitting at tin tables on blue and red plastic stools.

Loy speaks excellent English, which she acquired mainly through practice with foreigners. English has the distinction of being a lingua franca in the sex trade, although some of the women have now given priority to Japanese. Although, as Loy said, 'the only people who speak Japanese are Japanese'. She has a friend who learned Dutch from a boyfriend she stayed with for 18 months. Then the Dutchman went back home – 'to his wife' – and the friend was stranded, with a language she couldn't use with farangs. Loy said, 'I only go with English-speakers, because if you can talk, you have more advantages.' Loy was full of surprising insights. She said almost at the beginning of our conversation

Just as you get used to being young, you find out you are no longer young. It is a shock, a surprise. You see 17-year-olds, 18-year-olds and you realise that your time is nearly finished. Some people try to hide it, but you cannot. Then it is time to think of something else. No, if you do not think of it before then, it is already too late.

I don't know why, but I always thought about time. Maybe that sounds crazy; but at 21, 22, I could already see younger girls coming into the bars. And men are hungry for youth. You see their eyes eating up the girls. I started to save money. After the bars close at two o'clock, most girls are wide awake, they want excitement, they go out gambling or to eat, to have a good time. When the bars close, if you haven't been taken off, you can relax, enjoy the company of the other girls. You are not competing with them then, you are all sisters again. It is very good to pass time together, drink, tell stories, talk of the farangs, romance, the future, families, children.

But I never went out with them. I wanted to, but I wanted to save money more. Now I am over 30. I am ready to go home to my two children. I will open a beauty parlour, a shop, in Ubon, I don't know yet. I have enough to invest to make a living. To me, this is better than going abroad with some farang to a country you don't know. Many girls go and they come back after a few years, they have been beaten or have been abandoned, so they walk the streets in Hamburg or Stockholm. They have been in a cold and lonely country and they bring back that cold and that loneliness. I can always tell a girl who has been in Europe. I would never leave Thailand.

I have prepared for my life. They say, 'Oh, Loy is unusual. She is different.' They all used to come to me to read the love letters from their boyfriends, the promises to take them to America or Japan. So many promises broken, so many hearts. I never believed anything a man told me. I had many offers. But I would never leave my children. My boy is ten, my girl eight; already they are confused, they call my mother 'mother'. This is good. I left them with my parents because I know they love me and they will also love my children.

She shows me the pictures, wrapped in polythene, in a hand-bag full of make-up, jewellery, papers, ID card, condoms. The smudgy pictures show wooden walls, a flowering tree, two children surrounded by plastic toys, with Loy's mother and aunts in the background.

I do not think it is a good life but it is not bad either. I did not come from my village to do this work. I came to work in a garment house which was run by my mother's sister. I came with my cousins when I was 14. We stayed in Din Daeng, in a room above the workshop. I soon learned to use the machine – it is very simple work but so boring and backbreaking. So many hours looking at the wall, stitching shirts or pants, or the linings of jackets. My mother's sister looked after us. She gave us food and took care of us if we were sick. We went home at Song Kran, sometimes for the new year. I earned 100 baht a day, but we had to work from eight in the morning till ten or eleven at night.

My cousin didn't like it and she left. She used to go with my mother's sister to the market to look for work and there she met a foreigner, who worked in the market. He asked her to go with him and she did. He took her to restaurants and bars and she came and told me so many things. There is money to be made by beautiful girls in the bars. I didn't listen to her at first, but then, I felt so bored and unhappy, and I missed my home.

So I left my mother's sister and came to the bar. It was easy. One hundred baht for sitting at a machine until you were almost asleep – once I put some stitches in my finger because I was so tired – see, I still have the marks from that. And then 1000 baht for a couple of hours and dinner and maybe a hotel as well. It seemed like paradise. But it isn't. Many men are stupid and rude and sometimes they tell you they love you. It is work, but hard in a different way from the factory. The bar is a love factory, so it is the same. I thought I would make some money and then go back to Din Daeng, to the factory. But you cannot. You cannot go back.

We were such young girls when we came, we knew nothing of life. In Bangkok my education started. I guess if I had been from a better family, I would have had more schooling, I might have gone to university. I know that I have good sense. I could see many other women in the bar were just living for now and not thinking about what would happen to them. Tomorrow, prung nee, is another country for them, as though they will never reach it.

We had to fight to make sure the men wore condoms, because in the beginning, they thought it would spoil their pleasure or damage their manhood ... At first, management resisted, the customer is always right, but later, they understood that they have to keep the women in good condition, otherwise farangs will not come.

I have never gambled and I hate alcohol. I do not smoke. I have saved money and sent it to my mother. My mother's sister went home and told my mother what my sister and I were doing. I thought she would be angry, because I had told her I was working in a store. My sister died in 1993. She was very unhappy because she fell in love with a Thai man who was already married. He promised to leave his wife, he was always promising. She wanted to show him how much she loved him so he would go and live with her. She took some tablets, I do not believe she meant to do it, but she took too many and that night, he didn't come to her room. So the next day when she never arrived for work, he came to see me to find out if I knew what had happened. We found her lying as if she was asleep on the bed, but she was all stiff like wood and her face was cold and grey, as though she hated us.

I will never love; only my mother and father and my brother. I will not let this happen to me. I will have money. I will not suffer from love or poverty. Poverty made my mother old and my sister died of love. These are both dangerous things, worse than drugs, worse than sex work. Sometimes the spirit of my sister comes in the night; she has told me it is time to go home. Those who have died know things we do not and sometimes they come to us with their wisdom and we must listen.

VI

EMPOWER has a second office in the suburb of Nonthaburi and Chantawipa, founder of EMPOWER, is extending the work. She is a rare mixture of wisdom, tolerance and energy. I had first met her five years earlier, soon after EMPOWER had started. Since I last saw her, her awareness of the issues has deepened, and she perceives that the sex industry, the exploitation of poor women and the spread of AIDS cannot be separated from growing social inequality in Thailand. This calls into question the whole purpose and direction of 'development'.

Trafficking is under the control of the mafia, but the sex industry in Patpong is not, although the owners of course all know each other and they help each other with shared contacts in times of trouble. It is an industry and like all employers, they work the system – they know who can get fake papers through contacts in other countries, how to traffic women in and out. It is not like Yakuza gangs, but rather an informal network. They will know people at Immigration at the airport. It is not done from the top, it works informally – people will see a fake passport and, for a sum of money, they will let the holder through. They won't arrest the agent or trace back the passport to where it came from, but simply take the money and say nothing. We are still working in Patpong, but now we have this office also in Nonthaburi.

Nonthaburi is a suburb, about one hour by boat from the Harbour Department pier: a clock tower, crowded shopping and market centre; small vendors, selling everything from vegetables and fruits to plastic combs, buckets, cosmetics, watches, brushes, mops, hair ribbons, dresses, comic books, slices of watermelon, knives, chicken wings, buttons, cheap jewellery: it is a characteristic suburb, a mixture of urban poor and lower middle class.

The sex industry in this area is different from the international tourist area. Here, the brothels are often concealed by some other legitimate business; anyone who has a shop or small restaurant or beauty parlour may open up a brothel with ten or a dozen girls working. Or they start a karaoke bar. Some owners are musicians who play the electone, they get a machine and get employment in a place of entertainment. The women want to learn to sing, so he trains them. They can earn more if they also sing. The music players know how to make profit out of the women, which they sometimes share with them. The real owners, that is the landlords from whom the so-called owners rent, get most of the money.

This is a lower middle class area and there is a flourishing sex business: on the corner of all major streets, many bars and brothels, Thai traditional massage parlours. You can usually tell by the decoration if a business – a grocery store or something – is a front for a brothel. In the old days it was illegal to serve foreigners. Under the old monarchy, people used to give their daughters to people of higher rank; often maids and servants became mistresses, there was always the opportunity for promotion. My father, who is now 86, says that at that time there were dark corners where prostitution flourished, but there were not women employed on the scale and with the openness that we see today.

It has become more widespread and less clandestine in the past 30 years. During the Second World War the Japanese used women for prostitution; some Thai women were also taken to Japan as comfort women. The Japanese were brutal compared to the Americans who came in the 1960s and did it more sweetly, gave money. But it all contributed to the inferiorisation of Thais, it reinforced a sense of low status, a belief that wealth and power existed elsewhere. Many wanted to go abroad: to get a GI husband was the ambition of many young women. To stay close to privileged people was a Thai tradition which was easily transferred to foreigners when the old hierarchies of rank began to break down in Thai society. The rich *farang* is both a continuity and a radical break with the subservience of women to those of higher social standing. When people saw the royal family invite foreigners to teach their children, the missionaries came, and people thought the *farang* must have a superior status.

Thailand indirectly became a part of the Indo-Chinese war which left behind it a Western development culture – big dams, electricity for the military bases, the infrastructure of Bangkok, including the sex industry, all to serve the politics of destroying Communism. It destroyed a lot of other things as well, just as a herbicide kills all the medicinal plants along with the weeds. There was fear even here that the rural people would become Communists if they knew they were poor. Therefore, education was minimal. As though people need education to know they are poor! If people began to demand better food, housing, education, it would mean they had become Communists; so the government built roads to the so-called red and pink areas, in order to police them more effectively. This in turn confirmed a certain kind of development.

After the suppression of Communism in Thailand, they tried to control the people through family planning; they didn't want people to have so many children, because they thought too many hungry people would make trouble, so women were made to feel it was a fault if they had too many babies. Also they felt they were not modern: modernisation comes with militarisation. When the American military went, they left a whole culture behind, PX products, beer and cigarettes, gum; people were addicted to Western music, clothing, T-shirts and jeans, a whole culture which we accepted without ever asking why or whether it was appropriate. A sort of confusion which many of the young generation have inherited. They show the same addictions to Western consumer products as well as to computer games and cars from Japan.

At any one time there were 70,000 men in Bangkok for rest and recreation during the Vietnam war. The phenomenon of the *miachao*, the 'rented wife', was common; women hired for cleaning, washing and sex, all the most degrading elements rolled into one, a mixture of servant and

prostitute. This was the beginning of the rent-a-woman culture which has since become institutionalised in the sex
industry: the farangs come, pick up a woman, take her to
Phuket, Hong Kong or Malaysia. Women who tried to
empower themselves lost their jobs.

Many have no other skills. If they leave home and go to
work in entertainment, earn money, why not? Poor women
do not know the dangers of the sex industry. Most men
know of AIDS, they know that transmission is through nee-
dles, sex, homosex and heterosex; they know condoms help
to protect themselves and the women, but getting them to
use condoms in the sex industry is very difficult, especially in
an area like this. It is easier in the big international bars, but
in local bars there are still many who will not, because they
say it interferes with their pleasure.

AIDS. You don't die immediately, therefore it is not seen
as an immediate problem. People die of poverty, of poor
education; in factories their hand may be severed by machinery, in the chemicals industry they may inhale fumes while
making battery cells. They die in cars because there is no
safety. Those who work hardest die soonest of exhaustion.
They do not see people dying of AIDS; it means nothing, it is
just another – distant – problem on top of all the other social
problems.

How to change behaviour – that is the issue at all levels.
The rich will never give money to the poor. If the poor have
no rice, they will not eat bread, they say they are starving
because there is no rice. People do not change their habits
and behaviour as quickly as we think, as we would like; and
the same is true of sexual habits. To learn how to live with
it safely, so that we can get better health care, better education, better skills among the people – only that way can we
be saved from AIDS; or at least those who have it can live
longer. AIDS is not seen as an immediate danger by those
who must labour each day to survive.

In Uganda, where in places up to two-thirds of the people
are living with AIDS, they are still talking of prevention. We
will have a similar epidemic because those who control the
country do not see themselves as part of the problem. For
them the poor are the problem; which, in a way, is true,
because it is the poor who suffer from it most; but in the

long run, it does not spare even those who govern us. People die once; you don't die twice. AIDS is not genetically transmitted, but discrimination is genetic, because poverty is passed on from generation to generation. With AIDS, you die, it's over. But poverty goes on and that prepares another generation to suffer.

We have had to learn to live over the years with governments who are corrupt. We have to learn to live with the military who also over time have killed many thousands of individuals in many incidents and encounters; many people have disappeared. Similarly, we have to learn to live with AIDS.

Many people living with HIV are good educators. They have found meaning after HIV. People never tell others that they are poor or that they are ill. Yet with HIV, they become important. People talk about medicines, getting the money to go to the doctor, transport to go home. In other words, social disease precedes AIDS, the social diseases of poverty, unemployment, ignorance.

Those who cannot live with discrimination, they are the ones who die sooner. They die, not of disease, but they lose respect of other people and self-respect. They lose interest in life, they collude in their own death. They see AIDS as a killer and they succumb. Their life has already been devalued because of discrimination; they feel anger only at those who gave them the disease, not at the circumstances of their lives in which they become the most vulnerable – not only to AIDS but to all the other socially destructive forces at work.

Recently, there have been some attacks against a shelter for AIDS patients. This place has been attacked many times, stonings, fire-bombings. The shelter was really needed when it started; but it didn't work, because the community was not consulted, the people were not educated to accept it. The problem is not located in the community, or rather, they do not perceive it to be there. In a slum community, where people accept the existence of AIDS, they will acknowledge such a centre is needed, but this one was located in a commercial-residential area of small houses. It is not a community in the sense that we understand it in slums or in rural areas.

It may sound strange, but the lives of sex workers in the

*city are not so different from their lives at home: they know
each other as they would know their neighbours in the village. They see the same soap operas on TV, they are familiar
with the same commercial products. In Laos, too, they listen
to the Thai news and Thai music, their lives are articulated
to Thailand. There is little distinction between town and
rural life: the rural are not quite so penetrated by the market
culture but it only a question of degree. People cannot exercise their rights if they are poor and ill-educated, wherever
they live. Many poor people coming to Bangkok are even
more disadvantaged by the city – they can't read signs over
doors or on the streets, they cannot write down telephone
numbers. This means that are at risk from every form of
exploitation and discrimination.*

*Many people of higher social status and intellectuals who
have AIDS, they can live with it. But many street workers
have problems, which is why they come to us. We give them
condoms, try to teach them how to live with it, not to be
fatalistic, not to see it as a sentence of death. Others who
call us have mobile phones, they call from their cars because
they don't want anyone to know they are calling. They want
information. But the greatest problem is with those who
have no jobs or are powerless to get away from the risk of
the disease, girls in the sex industry; for those who work in
factories no social security is provided, nor for those who
work for a daily wage in construction as labourers. Those
people cannot go anywhere because to them to miss work is
to lose pay: they are the ones who suffer most, living with,
transmitting or receiving AIDS.*

*The educated know about transmission, they know what
to do, but they don't always do it. They think they can live
hidden, go on longer without telling anyone. They think: 'It
is not my disease, it is someone else's, I had bad luck.'*

*HIV people classify themselves, there is a hierarchy.
Those who got it through transfusions are the cleanest, the
least 'culpable', compared to others; then come drug users,
then homosexuals, with women sex workers at the bottom.
It is bad enough to be a sex worker, to be a sex worker who
is HIV-positive is worse. A man will say, 'I got it, I'm un-
lucky.' This man got the disease from a prostitute. She is
guilty. His wife is innocent, she gets it from her husband*

who got it from a sex worker. It is the sex worker who is
blamed for the whole chain, not the man. It is people in
poverty who are holding the problem of AIDS, on top of all
the other problems they are already trying to contain.

Even to begin to solve it, it will be necessary to provide
good health care for all. Jobs are what people with HIV need,
a livelihood that will not force them back into sex work, a
proper education. It is not 'prevention of AIDS' that needs to
be undertaken, but better standard of living, better education
and health care, higher skills, greater security for the poor
and marginal; without these things, we will not be able to
tackle the disease. It is simple: people must be lifted out of
poverty. As you know, the whole direction of development is
in the other direction – greater insecurity for the poor,
greater inequality. This is not the way it is going to change.

HIV people are now speaking out: not about curing it, but
about health care, education, research, as well as equal
rights and employment opportunities. In the beginning, no
one listened. People believed that AIDS was death; now it is
about life and how life is to be lived. Companies which
kicked people out when they were known to be HIV-positive
now keep them on. Improvements in health and safety at
work, this is what people need, protection not punishment.
It used to be said of leprosy that the curse of leprosy was life
not death; and there is a lesson for AIDS here, in that life is
not the curse but is the focus for social improvements. With
leprosy, you can separate the sufferers, but with AIDS you
cannot. HIV does not affect efficiency, you can be a lawyer,
artist, singer or taxi driver.

Because AIDS is related to human behaviour, people do
not wish to be criticised, therefore they remain silent. It is
an extension of sexually transmitted diseases – no one says,
'I have transmitted it', but 'I have a fever, I have caught it.'
AIDS is like having a broken heart – you cannot see it. It is
a test to human beings of what is wrong in human relationships. That is our challenge. It is not a test from God.

We have held workshops with teenagers. They told us that
their schools and colleges do not talk of AIDS prevention directly, nor of condoms, because their principal didn't like it.
We asked them, what other kinds of communicable disease do
you know? Scabies comes from dirt, it is something from out-

side. But things like herpes, sexually transmitted diseases – people do not wish to discuss them, not because these are communicable diseases but because they come directly from other people in ways that make transparent the relationship with those other people. It therefore always becomes somebody else's fault. 'What will you do with people who have AIDS?' The young people often say: 'Get them out, stay away from them, keep them separate, let them die.' Then we ask if any of the group has met anyone with AIDS: no one has. We say, 'If your friends have it, you will kick them out?' Then they start to think. 'Perhaps a relative at home. A brother or sister. What will you do if you find out?' Then they are quiet. Then we say, 'And if it was you?' Later, they will come to us and say they are sorry.

It is not just a question of condoms or giving out information, but the need to give education about human relationships. If we were to do so as a matter of course in our schools, it would solve so many other problems. But it is not on any curriculum. We are living in an information era, yet it is surprising what people do not know. There is so much information, there is much competition for getting people's attention, so much of commerce is striving to reach there first. It becomes very hard for young people to hack a path through the jungle of noise and sound in order to find human relationships. They know consumer goods, they know transnational products, they know how to recognise what they want; they don't know how to recognise each other's needs. Survival in the technological jungle has replaced survival in the real jungle which, for the most part, has been cut down.

We can't expect sex workers to change society. AIDS victims will not change it either. But they will ask for care, not out of pity, but as human beings who are equals.

Nonthaburi in the rain; great spreading puddles across the road, the home-going traffic reduced to a standstill. Crowds jostle; umbrellas tangled together on the sidewalk drag people into momentary unwilling proximity; they shake themselves free, laughing. An elderly man is driving a cycle-rickshaw. On his T-shirt is the message 'No One Knows I'm A Lesbian'.

6

STORIES FROM
A SEX INDUSTRY

I

The elderly woman works in a hotel. She wears a green smock and carries a dustpan and brush to sweep up the dust that collects in insubstantial grey curls and the cigarette butts that have left marks in the plastic floor covering. Her face is creased, her back slightly stooped. As she makes the beds in the room, the sheets form a white floating canopy in the air before coming to rest symmetrically on the base of the bed. Some of the mattresses beneath are stained, the ragged flowers of one form of incontinence or another.

Once she was in the bars, 20 years ago or more. She had plenty of boyfriends. Many Americans used to come then. They were generous. She had a baby with one of them, a little girl, half Thai, half American. Very beautiful. *Suay, suay.* But she worked in a bar. Her mother was in the village. She was sick. She could not leave the child with her. She gave her away to foreigners, people whom the American knew. They came to Bangkok, they came to the village. They were rich people. She didn't want to part from her baby, but what could she do? She had to look after her mother. The man and woman who took her, they got papers, everything was done properly. She received no money. She never heard from them after they disappeared with her child.

'Now I am old', she says, 'who will look after me?' Every baby she sees, she looks at, thinking it might have been her own. But of course she is now a grown woman. It is no use looking at babies, she would have to look at women in their mid-twenties; sometimes, when she sees a woman of mixed race, she wonders. But she would surely not come back from America; no one comes back from America. Does she even know she has a mother, a mother who thinks about her every day? The people who took her promised to write, to send pictures. Nothing came. The father went back to America. She never heard from him again. The tears in her eyes do not fall but spread in the wrinkles of her old face, forming a damp patch on the cheek.

II

The boy in the park works in a Bangkok bar. He is also an athlete. Every day he comes at twilight in his dark blue silk suit, strips down to a white singlet and pale blue shorts. He wheels and leaps into the air, exulting in the youth and energy of his body.

An old Chinaman sits on a concrete bench each evening when the young man is due; a skinny, skeletal figure, leaning on a stick. The boy never looks at him but stares straight ahead as though absorbed by his daily practice. The old man looks at him with an intensity that equals the boy's efforts to avoid his gaze. The athlete nevertheless seems to seek a greater perfection under the eye of the unacknowledged spectactor. He folds his clothes carefully; every gesture is an elegant sketch of his own self-conscious pride, the triumph of the young over the old, the only wisdom they have, which is to have been born later than those whose life is nearly over.

The boy has a self-possession and completeness, as now his right arm, now his left, touches the sky and the other one grazes the soggy newly watered grass. Scented frangipani flowers, the purple of a rose of India strew the ground where he jumps and turns. From time to time, he leaves the neat pile of clothing and runs around the perimeter of the garden. The old man keeps a watchful eye on the little heap of blue silk on the grass, as if he had been appointed custodian of the uninhabited clothes, even though there is no question that anyone would take them. The boy returns and sinks to the ground. He lies exhausted, his chest rising and falling with his breath; the soft mound of his genitals the centre of his sprawled body.

One day the old man does not come. For once, the boy scans the horizon. He does not come. Nor the next day. The boy looks searchingly now. The old man does not come to the park again. If there is less of a spring in his leap, if his gestures are a little more careless, who is to notice it? One day, he walks over to the bench where some other elderly men are sitting. 'Who was the old man?' he asks, indicating the empty stone bench beside the ornamental lake. 'Just an old Chinese who died', they say indifferently. After that, the boy never again returns to the same spot in the park for his practice, but chooses a place as far away from it as he can find.

III

He says his name is Peter. A Dane, in his early thirties, with curly fair hair, wearing blue shorts and a T-shirt. A hot afternoon in September, between showers of rain; pink and bronze clouds cast a curious metallic light over the park, while evaporation from the puddles is visible in the vapour from the ground that rises up as though from subterranean fire. This is his first visit to Thailand where he is on a six-month work contract. He finds the sex industry repelling. He hates the bars, they appear to him, he says, hellish, garish colours, the women white as corpses in the strobe lights, the music strident and deafening.

He had picked up a young woman on the street. She was a shop worker in Central Department Store. She was plainer than the women in the bars, but she had a nice smile. Peter thought he would rather get to know someone who was not involved in the bars. He took her for a meal. The next day, they went to the serviced apartment which the company he works for retains permanently for its representatives in Thailand. They had a pleasant evening. He thought he might see her again. This would make for agreeable diversions from his busy schedule. But she didn't see it like that at all. He says she fell in love with him.

She would not leave the flat. For a few days, it was all right. Then she didn't want me to go to work. She stopped going to Central Store. After about a week, I realised that not only did I not love her, but I didn't even want her. I didn't want her around, she was so clinging, it was as though her life depended on me. I said, 'I don't know you, you don't know me.' Her English was not good, but she kept saying 'I love you. You never leave me. I stay with you. I am your wife.' I grew to resent her. This was not part of the deal. I even stopped liking her. I didn't want to touch her. I thought maybe she was just saying this, so that I would take her home with me, I thought she was scheming perhaps. But I soon realised that she was a desperate woman. I was frightened. The more I tried to tell her I didn't love her, the more she wept and clung to me. I became angry. It didn't make any difference.

In the end, I waited one day until she went out to get some food. Then I left the apartment and checked into a hotel. I'm still there. I lived in fear of running into her, although I went to work by car. I would not go out in the evening. Then I wondered what would happen because I had left her in the apartment on her own. She said she would kill herself. I could imagine her body being discovered by the cleaning staff. I thought I would be accused of murder and thrown into jail.

After four days, I couldn't bear the worry of it. I went back. My heart was beating as I turned the key in the lock. I didn't know what I would find. The place was empty. She had written something in Thai in lipstick all over the wall and a picture of a figure that looked as though it was hanging from a tree. I asked one of the staff to translate it for me. It was some kind of curse, saying that she would follow me into my next life. I thought as long as she doesn't bother me in this one any more, I could bear it. But this spoiled it for me. I'm still in the hotel. I won't go back to the apartment. And I won't come back to Thailand.

IV

Bangkok is a great keeper of secrets despite the display and show. Westerners think that sex is the ultimate authentic human experience. The young women and men of Bangkok know better. Because the farangs are so lonely, because they are such isolated individuals, they imagine that it is through sex that human beings come closest to one another. They think they see the profoundest communication in what is the loneliest experience in the world. They think like this because they are so far away from each other, they have to reach across the empty spaces of their separateness before they can touch another human being.

It is difficult for the young women and men in the sex industry. It is not that the constant mauling and penetration by strangers does not reach them: to be subjected to continuous assault in this way must have its effect. But for them, sex certainly does not have the same transcendent significance that it has for many of their Western clients. The core of their being, their spirit, may remain less impaired by all the physical handling and manipulation than sex workers from other cultures which have been more profoundly damaged, or at least, influenced, by Western dominance. Where the farangs look to sex for the greatest authenticity of which they believe human beings are capable, the Thais remain – perhaps – less disturbed by the turbulence which, to some extent, passes over them. This is why many of their farang clients accuse them of dishonesty. For the farang sex is deadly serious; not a game.

Of course, there are many abused, unhappy and despairing women in the sex industry: but not all are victims. They are not all damaged personalities, any more than they are all merely workers who just happen to be doing this job rather than working in a factory or as domestic workers.

When I suggested this at a meeting at the University of Leicester in June 1996, one woman, a former sex worker in Bradford, disagreed strongly. She insisted that all women are wounded, damaged by such experiences. Was she right, or was this another example of projecting our dominant Western experience on to others? Can we assume the universal applicability of our perceptions on all societies? Or is the assertion that Thai sex workers may be less harmed by their work than those from other cultures, merely an unwitting piece of special pleading, the propagation of a myth that sex tourists want to hear? I really don't know.

V

The foreigner is taken home, he thinks, to meet the family. This must be a sign that he is accepted, absorbed into the family body. In spite of the discomfort of spending the night on a mat on the wooden floor, the cockroaches and rats, the cold water, the rice three times a day, the coarse local drink, the curiosity of the villagers whose language he cannot understand, he thinks, 'At least I am accepted.' What he doesn't know is that the woman has perhaps taken him home to show her family why she is doing what she does. He thinks it's a courtship ritual whereas he is being shown as a status symbol. She is bringing the separate worlds of work and home together; for her, it is an attempt at integration. So afterwards, when it becomes clear that he is expected to extend his generosity to the wider family, he is bound to think his generosity and kindness have been abused; and she won't be able to understand his anger.

VI

Tian, 25, a receptionist at a gay club, receives no salary, only the tips from customers who take him off. He says 25 is a terrible age for a gay boy. You are finished. No customer for ten days. But then he smiles. A Japanese gave me 1000 baht for a short time. The Japanese give most money. Tian knows English. He says he ought to have studied Japanese. 'A young guy from Singapore gave me 800 baht to fuck him.' I asked if he wore a condom. 'No, he was good looking, my age; he didn't have AIDS. I don't care anyway. Sometimes I want to die.' He makes a gesture of cutting his throat. 'They want younger men; and Bangkok is full of them.' Too old at 25, the tinted hair, the teeth spoiled by early malnutrition, the creases around the eyes. He says I have smiled too much.

VII

Speaking of the scrupulous cleanliness of Thais in general and of his boyfriend in particular, the farang complains, 'He even makes me clean my teeth before he'll let me take his cock in my mouth.'

VIII

She comes from Isan where their 20 *rai* of land is flooded by the heavy rains. 'Home washed away', she says, making a sweeping gesture like water.

I live with my sister. Her husband is Chinese. He left her. Somebody fed a charm into his drink and he forget everything, forget his two babies, forget his wife. Farang not believe. I thought I cannot work in a bar. I too shy to take off my clothes and be go-go dancer. My friend works as hairdresser, she tells me to train, then I get 10,000 baht a month, meet film stars, maybe find someone to take me away. But a bar, you don't have to do anything. Just look good. I have a boyfriend who is a Frenchman. I love him but I do not like him. I do not want to see him, but when he comes to Bangkok, I cannot refuse him. He takes me to the Dusit Thani hotel, big meals, drinking. He is boring me.

Boring, it isn't that. I have been bored, I can take it. But farangs, why do they have to show everything? Our women show their bodies, but they show every feeling, it is horrible. He gets angry and he shouts at the taxi driver, he screams at the waiter, he orders the woman in the shop what she must do. Oh he says he loves me. I say to him 'I do not love you' and then he cries like a woman. I say to him, 'Why are you like a lady-boy?' I do not show that I do not like him. Why are Europeans like this, can you tell me? They keep nothing inside. We can tell by a look in the eye if we are feeling bad, but we keep it inside. I cannot tell him for a long time. This is my work and this is my money. He pays money. But I do not want him to show what he feels, when I cannot say anything that I am feeling inside.

I think it is selfish and like a child, not a grown man. And because I do not say anything, he thinks I love him too. So he is very surprised when I say, 'I do not love you.' He cries. But he is so crazy for me, he does not hear what I say. I do not want him. I give him to my friend in the bar, but he comes back to me. I cannot help it. I cannot tell him. I feel repulsion for him, because he does not see me, he does not know me. He does not know who I am, he just sees my body and feels his own desire and for him I am an empty person, I do not exist, so he just fills me with what he is feeling.

IX

Until last week, or last month at the latest, Bangkok must have been a ghost city; because all the beautiful young women, and all the sweet young men, have only just arrived; perpetually new to the city, they have not yet been ruined by it. Theirs is a life of constant new starts, fresh pages, relationships just begun; a constant renewal of hope, even when they know that

the city devours their friends and the people they came with
from the village. By saying they have just arrived, they wipe out
all the disagreeable experiences.

X

One boy who works in a bar told me why he will not work
in industry, why he prefers the sex trade. He had some
friends who died in a factory. Two young men were cleaning
a deep concrete trough which was used for mixing mangoes
to make preserves. They were playing a radio which was
plugged into the electric socket which drove the machinery
and suddenly everything went quiet; they had been electro-
cuted. Nobody knew what had happened. Another friend
went to investigate and he never came out; so a fourth went
in and he too was killed; the metal had become live.

XI

'There is no man living', says Seri vehemently, 'who is so old,
so ugly, so disagreeable, whose flesh hangs in repulsive folds,
whose breath smells worse than the fumes on Rama IV, who
does not, somewhere in his mind, believe that he is lovable.'
This is the Thai woman's secret. This is why she will pick the
most unattractive feature, the baldness, the paunch, the droop-
ing *kueh* and make it the object of her particular attention; as
though the most ugly aspect of him were what she most ad-
mires. It is irresistible. There is no man who will not melt
under this kind of flattery. Other women maybe in other countries will choose not to look at the worst thing about a man,
will pretend it doesn't matter. A Thai woman will go straight
for the most vulnerable part and say this is what she loves.

XII

Od, 22, from Petchabun, came to Bangkok two years ago,
when he saw an advertisement in a newspaper for boys
wanted for bar work. He came alone, did not know it was a
gay bar. He was told by one of the other boys what was
expected of him. He worked for three months as a go-go
dancer and then gave it up because he found he could do
better as a freelancer, working in a hotel bar on weekdays
and in Lumpini Park at weekends. His father died two years
ago of a brain haemorrhage caused by drink. His mother

farms ten *rai* of land, his brother works as a labourer on a
building site at home, earning 200 baht a day (8 US dollars).
Od is not gay. It is work. He has many friends, women
working in the bars. He says he intends to save up 30,000
baht (1200 US dollars) and go back home, marry a girl from
his village and open a video store there. Od's skill lies in his
ability to make love with those whose sexual orientation he
does not share. It does not bother him. Does he think of
women? He says I think of the money, 1000 baht for a
night, two or three customers a week. I always carry a condom. Someone told him that if a woman in Cambodia is
found carrying a condom, she can be arrested, because to
carry a condom proves she is a prostitute.

Od is a perfectly ordinary young man, white T-shirt, blue
jeans; yet he says he could never be a mason like his
brother, nor a farmer like his father. Why? 'I could not do
it.' What has given him the sense of another destiny, separate from his siblings? Where does the idea come from that
he is special, different? He smiles, a secret knowing smile,
the smile of someone who has a secret rendezvous.

XIII

In the clubs you cannot tell what epic dislocations and losses
have driven them here. The woman who is smiling, wearing a
fluorescent white bikini, her father is in prison for murder,
having killed someone after a game of cards: she is now the
only support of a family of seven. The man with the thin
sculpted face who fucks men for a living, what dark revenge is
he seeking against the stepfather who kept him locked up in a
cupboard for six months when he was five years old, while he
listened to this man and his mother make love on the floor of
their hut in Korat?

XIV

The woman is reading a letter from her boyfriend in America.
He lays out his conditions for marriage and her move to the
US. 'You will have to do as I say and obey me. I do not want to
take care of all your family. If you accept my conditions, you
will have a nice house and a car and a good life. Send me some
pictures of yourself, sexy ones, also some sexy pix of your
sister.'

XV

A man in the Suriwong hotel is buying breakfast for his boy
and for two of the boy's friends. They order everything on
the menu, joking and talking Thai. The foreigner, maybe
Dutch, in his late sixties, becomes increasingly anxious but
he continues to smile. The table is soon piled with beer
bottles, orange juice, noodles, eggs, fish, rice. They smile at
him, he smiles back. The bill comes to 1500 baht. He pays.
The boys do not thank him but get up, run out into the
courtyard, laughing and chattering like children released from
school at playtime. The man is left counting the banknotes
in his wallet.

XVI

'She started talking about going to the jewellers on my second morning in Bangkok. I thought Christ, what is this, a
marriage proposal? I didn't know then that gold is a symbol
of security, they buy it and sell it and as long as they have a
couple of chains round their neck they're at least two steps
from destitution.'

7

THE SEX INDUSTRY BECOMES
THE AIDS INDUSTRY

The Thai Ministry of Public Health estimated the number of HIV-positive people in Thailand at 650,000 in July 1994. That is about one per cent of the population. The number of AIDS patients is around 6000. The Ministry estimated that the HIV-positive figures are likely to rise to between two and four million by the end of the century.

Those groups which have been affected tell a story which shows that this affliction, like almost every other, claims the poorest first. In Thailand, originally detected amongst injecting drug users, those who had received transfusions of contaminated blood, female and male prostitutes, it spread to their (mostly) male clients. These are, for the most part, migrant labourers, people uprooted to feed the industrialising of Thailand. These took the infection back to their villages, to their wives and subsequently, to their own children. In some places, up to 30 per cent of 'low-charge' female prostitutes have been affected, that is, those who service poor Thai men, labourers, migrants, construction workers. The 'high-charge' prostitutes who work in bars, nightclubs and massage parlours are more rigorously monitored; if they become affected, they are dismissed.

In spite of government health programmes and growing awareness of the issue, consciousness reaches the most needy last of all. This is not only a consequence of 'ignorance' or a lack of education: it is also a result of the more urgent pressures of life upon the poorest, the need for a sex worker to pursue her livelihood, even if this undermines life itself. One woman who has worked with prostitutes for ten years contrasted the slowness of the growth of understanding among the poor about AIDS with the facility with which even the most wretched can name brands, recognise logos, identify transnational consumer products. She said: 'This demonstrates the priorities of society: knowledge of what to do for survival is subordinate to familiarity with commercial advertising.'

There is also evidence – much of it admittedly anecdotal and not easily researched – of a certain recklessness among HIV-positive foreigners who come to Thailand. I met one man from the US who said he had come to Thailand because he didn't care whom he infected here. 'It's no concern of mine. If they ask me to use a condom, I will, if not, what is it to me? I've nothing to lose.' The racism inherent in sex tourism becomes more transparent in such cases, more punitive: those who fear for their own lives have little compunction about seeking a kind of vengeful fellowship in their suffering; but it is significant that they are inhibited from such behaviour at home.

Dr Vithit Mantabhorn of the Department of Law, Chulalongkorn University, has been actively involved in the campaign against child prostitution and at the same time has been a persuasive advocate for those affected by AIDS. He says that the most obvious impact has been the public lack of understanding of, and sympathy for, those with the disease.

The disease wreaks havoc with the poorest, especially in the Northern provinces. They are not only denied basic necessities of life, but on top of this they have the burden of the economic costs of HIV/AIDS: the loss of a breadwinner, family break-up, children orphaned; children of parents who are HIV-positive are often abandoned, shunned or discriminated against. There is a rise in the number of cases where hospitals and doctors refuse to care for HIV patients and employees of companies have been dismissed. This is all made worse by the lack of a comprehensive social security system in Thailand to care for the most disadvantaged. One estimate of the economic cost to Thailand is 9 billion US dollars by the year 2000; care and assistance for each individual cost between 40,000 and 70,000 baht.

Vithit Mantabhorn recommends the setting up of a state social security system to help those with the disease; voluntary testing by business of its employees; drugs subsidised by government to bring treatment within reach of the poor; promotion of community care, with a role also for religious institutions in caring for those affected; use of national and local funds to help the needy and their families; broader public education to counter the use of the sex trade and to promote responsible male behaviour; eradication of criminal networks which exploit women and children for sexual purposes, by means of both better law enforcement and community participation; access by women to more effective precautions, such as the female condom; provision of alternative family care for HIV/AIDS orphans and abandoned children; training and use of grandparents and other relatives as substitute parents for children whose parents are affected; and the involvement of those with HIV/AIDS who wish to participate in media campaigns to inform the public.

Many who campaign for better treatment – both social and medical – for HIV-positive people, speak of the need for a social security system such as exists in the West. It is a poignant and bitter experience to return to Britain and hear all politicians not only talking about cutting welfare provision but also invoking countries like Thailand, where the strength of the family and 'social cohesion' are supposed to be more effective than expensive welfare systems.

Greg Carl is an American, working as AIDS Co-ordinator with the Thai Red Cross. The office is in a corner of a sizeable compound on Rama IV Road, not far from Patpong, centre of the sex industry. There is also a free anonymous STD clinic. Greg Carl has observed the sex industry and the spread of HIV in the West and has a clear view of both the similarities and the differences in the way it has been dealt with in Thailand.

Commercial sex in the West now tends more and more to be related to drug use – it is increasingly a way of raising

money for the fix. Here, it is not like that. In the West the
sex industry is more controlled, more violent. In Thailand it
remains more emotionally based, that is, less mechanistic,
even though many people enter the sex industry to support
themselves and their families. It is, in that sense, a sacrifice
on the part of women. Sex workers do seek close relationships with their clients; and that also differentiates them
from most Western sex workers. They want a relationship as
well as an income and maintenance for the family. There
are few professions to equal the potential earnings for
women. If she settles with one man, the problem arises,
how does he help the whole family unless he is very rich?
Foreigners will support them to a certain extent, but they
can rarely provide the level required for the woman's
dependants.

The image of the West is of broken values. Thai culture is
like that of the West as it was 40 years ago, when a man
was expected to look after his wife and family. In the West
now, that responsibility is shared. In Thailand, either you
give or you accept responsibility. The father is supposed to
be responsible for the family, for everything. Now, with the
uprooting, migration, industrialisation, families break: it may
be the father who stays home while the mother comes to
Bangkok, or both mother and father may migrate to different
provinces. Yet the expectations in terms of roles and responsibilities remain: there is a time lag between the actual social and economic change and the social consequences of
these; and this can be disorienting, disturbing, dangerous. So
sex workers, in spite of working in these sleazy places, in
spite of the tacky glamour and the lights and music, want
someone to be responsible for them.

The development model imported from the West is a package. Unless jobs and education opportunities increase, it will
become like the West here. In North America, young people
can get an education and they don't mind working to earn it.
Here, there is a status-oriented culture. A priority here would
be, in my estimation, to change the status system: status
becomes frozen, like that of many academics who did research
ten years ago and live off the name they made then, and no
one contradicts them. If I could change one thing in Thai
society, this would be it.

Here, at the Red Cross, we keep our information confidential. We collect, but we don't report to anyone else. The Ministry of Public Health publishes estimates which are lower than we believe the reality to be. They do a biannual surveillance of regional offices, survey direct and indirect sex workers, STD cases, antenatal clinics, military conscripts – a cross-section of the population at risk – and then projections are calculated from these. Actually no one quite knows where the statistics come from; the Ministry does not reveal how they are arrived at. There is no systematic analysis. In fact, it only really matters in terms of getting foreign money, in terms of the law and social policy. As far as intervention goes, numbers are not important – it is the quality of the intervention that counts.

Early on, the target populations were assumed to be mainly gays and drug users, so nobody else had to worry. This assumption came up with consistently low figures. There is no easily monitorable gay culture in Thailand. There is a gay culture, but it is not easily reached by official scrutiny. In any case, gay sex workers are mainly heterosexual, so it is all more complicated.

Many of those who are HIV-positive or people with AIDS say they just want to die. They see it as a death sentence. They simply want to get through this life and on to the next one; it is part of the cycle of rebirth, finish with this one as quickly as possible. It has to be acknowledged that this does offer some consolation to people; the culture gives them a form of hope which those who do not believe in a future life are denied. This is more so in the rural population of course. In the urban areas, the psyche is more materialistic. In the countryside, people are more attached to their family, more rooted in religious custom, whether Buddhist or animist.

At first, the official campaign against AIDS consisted of scare tactics which had negative effects. This relegated it to the realm of fate; it meant trying to appease the demon, not get rid of it. People affected do have support groups in places like Bangkok and Chiang Mai; they feel they have an important role, helping one another and also educating others and spreading an understanding. In the North and Northeast the support groups are not there.

In Nonthaburi recently a centre for HIV/AIDS people was bombed. A second centre was also attacked. The problem was that the hospice was set up without any attempt to provide education for those living in the neighbourhood. People didn't understand. It takes something like these attacks to make people think. A new centre is to be set up in Galaxy Soi (this is a street of commercial sex establishments) for those losing their jobs and houses through HIV. A commercial sex establishment owns the soi (street). They are wondering how it will be received – some education, some PR is necessary. People going to a soi for commercial sex will see the centre that serves HIV/AIDS; it will make them think, but will it put them off the sex business? That is the question. Some bars – notably the King's Group – have their own medical facility where the workers are tested weekly, although this can give a false sense of security. In Thailand the policies on secrecy of HIV status are only guidelines, not law as in the West. There is still no control over the window period – the three to six months when someone who is infected can still be working; it shows up only after a certain time lag.

Generally, those with sexually transmitted diseases are supposed to be on hold, but some carry on working because they believe that once they start the medication, they will be safe. In one bar, there was a young man affected and still working. The other boys said to the owner, 'Why don't you remove him?' The owner said, 'He'll only go to another bar. If he stays here, at least we can keep an eye on what he does.'

There is a hierarchy of sex workers. Those in the massage parlours and the high-class call girls are at the top. People tend to tumble down the ladder, according to age, marketability and, of course, health. If they are dismissed from one place, they go elsewhere where there are fewer questions asked.

With male sex workers, they tend to play safe with the customers, but what happens if the client offers more money to do it without a condom? On the whole, the male workers work together to diminish the risk of infection. You can't always know whether they are gay: they tend to act butch, because this is generally what the punters want. Many of the young men are also helping their families, just as the women are. There is little help available for male sex workers.

Because men have more opportunities generally and are privileged, they are less likely to be the object of official attention. Those male sex workers who are gay see gay culture as a lot of short-lived relationships that bring unhappiness. What they want is a long-term loving, steady relationship. Yet this seems impossible, so they settle for short-term attachments for money.

Many sex workers come into the job as they would go into any other – through contacts with brothers, sisters, cousins. It is seen as doing them a favour to get them work, as if it were in a factory or workshop. One of the saddest things they all say is that the first time they do it, they experience fear, terror of the customer. They are very nervous and find it hard to go through with it; but then after some time, they take it in their stride and eventually do it as they would any other job. It is largely play-acting. We in the West accept our body and our self as a whole. The Asians do not. The sex workers say 'I sell my body, not my heart.' This can mean many things, they do not sell their being or their spirit. In our culture, we live in the mind, which is inseparable from the body. In Thailand these are split entities; because the spirit is reborn again and again, it cannot be reached, damaged, touched.

They are influenced by the hardness of the city compared to the village. There is the enticement of material goods, clothing, consumer items. In the village, kids may share a school uniform, go to school in it on alternate days; but once here, they get hooked on keeping up their image, the needs become greater. They get addicted to cards, gambling, fashion, motorbikes. On the other hand, there is a carry-over of the tradition of mutual help from the people up-country. People do share, they replicate family and sibling structures even with strangers in the city; they give to those who do not have; whereas the middle-class Bangkok people are less willing to spend their wealth. The country people spend, they don't save; they see money as an agent that enables them to get through life, not as something to be accumulated.

The sex industry is probably a net cost to Thailand. It compels people to do things against their will and against their nature. There is too little control by sex workers over decision-making. It is a form of servitude, especially for women. They borrow money from the bars and become bonded to the owners. Above all, those who are sold or trafficked never receive any of the money. There are some very private clubs and brothels where the women remain virtual captives. If they get sick, it can be costly; a boy may get 200 baht from a punter and then have to pay 600 baht for a gonorrhoea shot.

Moreover people in Thai society do not express emotion. It is often very lonely for those who come to the city. People find it difficult to reach out to each other and this is perhaps why the longing for someone is so pervasive, even among sex workers. This is very different from the relationships embedded in family and kinship structures: this is the anguish of transition, if you like, becoming urban, learning how to live in a different way.

To add to this, you get all these people coming from abroad, many of whom have failed relationships at home; and they, too, are reaching out. They may convince themselves they want to save a young woman from the sex scene; but it is a tangle of romantic, social and economic needs on both sides that make it such a confusion. They may discover they cannot rescue each other, but they may be able to rescue themselves. Previously, the power was all with the customers; but since AIDS/HIV have become so prominent, the owners have had to co-operate with the Public Health Department, become more flexible, give more freedom to the sex workers to negotiate with customers.

Most Thai women work very hard within the family. Perhaps this is why they say they are looking for someone to take care of them – so they can take care of him. They are looking for security within an exploitative relationship. The sex trade is a form of slavery in which women are free to look for a relationship that will enslave them at another level.

8

THE SEX MARKET
AND HUMAN RIGHTS

I

The sex trade is exactly that: supply and demand, a perfect paradigm of the market economy. Those who speak of the market economy as though it represented the highest achievement in the organisation of human affairs – some even see in it the hidden hand which belongs, presumably, to Providence, or God – often fail to recognise that it does not obligingly cease its operations at the frontiers of decency, honour and good sense. Some of the most dynamic markets in the world deal in illicit goods and substances – arms, pornography, gold, drugs, ivory and other products from protected animals, children and their labour, trees, diamonds and flesh, for example. Here is a real enterprise culture, one that throws back to those prophets of the universal market an unflattering reflection of their rosy version of the world.

By 1995, for the first time, a majority of migrant workers in the world were women. In countries with 'surplus' populations, many governments have a policy of labour export. It is estimated that about 18 per cent of families in the Philippines depend upon remittances for their survival; while the Labour Minister of Indonesia in 1995 expressed his hope that the number of Indonesians working abroad would reach two million by the turn of the century, which would produce 10 billion dollars for the country.

Thailand has pursued a policy of exporting labour since 1977; originally, overwhelmingly male and to the Gulf. The

numbers of men going abroad have fallen, while the demand
for women, especially as domestic labour and in cleaning
services, but also as nurses and child-carers has continued to
rise. An increasing proportion – officially and unofficially –
go as entertainers, or sex workers. Migration for the purposes
of prostitution is not legal anywhere and this makes women
vulnerable to extreme exploitation. It provides work, however, for the growing syndicates of traders, dealers and traffickers in women.

A characteristic example of trafficking was reported in
Bangkok in October 1995. A Japanese national and a Thai
citizen were charged with 'illegally exporting Thai women to
Japan with counterfeit documents'. (The reporting here – in
the *Bangkok Post* – is significant: the counterfeit documents
seem to be the focus of the objection rather than the nature
of the merchandise!) 'The suspects were arrested in a rented
apartment room in Klong Toey. Acting on a tip-off, a team
of Immigration Division police searched the room and found
a number of forged papers: no fewer than 22 items of forged
documents, 65 fake passports, 34 copies of ID request forms,
6 copies of household registration forms, 5 copies of divorce
certificates, 6 copies of company registration certificates and
seals of various districts and office heads. Police said the
gang was behind the procurement of sex workers from Thailand to Japan under the guise of a registered company. The
company had allegedly arranged fake travel documents and
visas for Thai women wanting to work as prostitutes in
Japan and charged each woman between 35,000 and 60,000
baht for its services.'

Trafficking is not new. Ever since the Bowring Treaty of
1855, forced by Britain upon Thailand to end its isolation
and to open the country to international trade, Chinese
labour was imported into Thailand to facilitate the transition from self-reliance to production for the market. To
service this male labour, many women and children came
to Thailand – some recruited forcibly – for marriage or
prostitution. The traffic in human beings has become both
more lucrative and more complex in the last two decades.
All over the world, borders are now closing, especially in
Europe. This is partly a consequence of mass unemployment in countries which, until the 1980s, had received

large numbers of migrants from the South, ostensibly 'to do the jobs nobody else wanted to do', but more realistically to create a pool of surplus labour, in an effort to keep down wages. This has been particularly successful in the USA, where millions of unofficial economic migrants, some of them risking their lives crossing the Rio Grande in search of a better life, have accepted lower and lower rates of pay, which have conspicuously driven down labour costs over the past 15 years.

The integrated global economy has at least one major flaw. While 'free trade' permits the growing mobility of both capital and goods, no such liberalisation is extended to human beings. It is not to be expected that this – to the poor, arbitrary – restriction on one element of wealth creation, one factor of production, should be accepted without a struggle. And indeed, world-wide, people seek to evade it and often succeed in doing so. It is in this context that trafficking in women flourishes. Women have become like many other restricted commodities in the world – the objects of flourishing unofficial markets.

The attraction for labour to travel from the impoverished places in the Third World is inscribed in the universal iconography of wealth and luxury transmitted to even the smallest villages by the global media. This makes it all the easier for traffickers to exploit young country people, those who have seen industrial life only through the TV screen and who are not aware of the exploitation concealed by the glamorous images which bombard them from childhood. The eagerness of young women to go abroad, to travel, to seek work beyond the borders of their village or country, leads them into the arms of those who will entrap them and keep them in bondage or slavery for sexual purposes.

There has been a change in the patterns of migration, according to the Friends of Women Foundation in Bangkok. Rural poverty fed the first wave of migration to the cities in the 1960s. Young women went to the city and there often found their way into the sex industry, falling under the control of pimps and recruiters. This was especially true of the period of the Vietnam war. By the 1970s, enough young women had returned to the villages with

money to make sex work more or less 'respectable', or at
least desirable, and many women came to Bangkok and
other towns and resorts in Thailand to work in the bars
and clubs. It was only in the 1980s that the recruiting and
trafficking of young women and girls became industrialised,
systematised by local and foreign traffickers, whereby the
women were directly recruited in the villages for purposes
of prostitution. They were – and continue to be – duped,
enticed with promises of regular and rewarding work in
shops, restaurants, or as domestic workers.

In the 1990s, even this pattern has undergone another
change. The stories of girls kidnapped or deceived into prostitution are now reaching some of the rural areas, either from
women who have escaped from forced prostitution in Japan
or elsewhere, or through the work of NGOs in the villages.
Awareness of the fate of country women in some parts of
Thailand has now alerted a new generation to the dangers of
being recruited for glamorous jobs in distant places. As a
result, the focus of the trade is now shifting to women from
ethnic minorities, especially the northern hill tribes in Thailand and Cambodia, Burma, Laos and China, who remain
unaware of what is waiting for them on the other side of the
promises.

Trafficking has evolved out of the routes followed by sex
tourists; in the 1970s and 1980s many young women
finished up in Western Europe, especially Germany, Netherlands and Scandinavia; Japan, too, is a well travelled destination for Thai and Southeast Asian women. There is evidence
that some who came to Thailand as sex tourists have taken
women as 'brides', and then set them to work in the sex
trade in Europe. The move to direct recruitment in remote
areas was given additional impulse by the fear of AIDS and
the 'market' for women free of infection. Networks of co-
operation between traffickers exist: go-betweens in the village
areas, recruiters at national level and international criminal
gangs.

It should not be thought that it is the lure of gain or
'bright lights' that drives young women away from home.
The story is more complicated and goes deeper than that. A
whole pattern of development, whereby small farmers and
rural areas are inadequately rewarded for their labour, the

enclosure and use of land for industrial purposes, deforestation and degradation of land, underlie a rural impoverish-
ment, which led many men to migrate in the 1960s and
1970s, both nationally and internationally. Many of these
paid recruiters and middlemen and incurred debts they could
not repay; and a considerable proportion of young women
later embarked on this unknown path for the sake of revers-
ing a situation made hopeless by earlier male migrations
from the home-place: the role of sex workers as redeemers
only adds to the burdens and pressures upon them.

Nor do the countries of destination for trafficked women
make it easy for them to escape from their situation. Some
women – especially those from Thailand who have been refu-
gees, or are from minority groups and do not have Thai
identity cards – become stateless persons. Others become
objects of racial discrimination and violence and are on the
receiving end of punitive and coercive action from the state if
they are discovered. Laws and prohibitions on prostitution in
both the sending and receiving countries conspire to deny the
human rights of the women abducted and sold into slavery.
This makes them more dependent upon their captors and
more likely to endure all kinds of indignities rather than
throw themselves on the mercy of the authorities of a country whose language they frequently cannot speak and whose
customs they do not know. They are often threatened with
jail by those who control them if they should try to run
away. Many young women, ostensibly recruited for work in
the catering industry, restaurants, hotels or as domestic
workers, find themselves as bonded prostitutes, with no
rights, no limit on the hours of work, no control over their
bodies and at risk from HIV infection and other sexually
transmitted diseases. They are blamed for an illegal status
which they never sought: often they have been tricked by
false marriages, they have gone abroad as mail order brides,
as maids or nannies. The Foundation for Women proposes
that the UN Convention on Traffic in Persons and the
Exploitation of Prostitution of Others 1949 should cover all
current forms of trafficking in women.

Again, the wider context of economic 'development' has had
a determining role in all this. The abuse of human rights is
written into a global system which has, as a consequence, a

growing inequality between rich and poor. With deeper market penetration of the lives of the people, those whose earning capacity cannot keeep pace are simply excluded from participation. The denial of economic rights, particularly in a developmental model that is intensively and exclusively dependent on money, is a potential and actual abuse of human rights. Human rights that do not include the right to livelihood and hence, the right to survival, are an inadequate formulation of those rights. Correspondingly, as the rights of the poor are curtailed, the rights of the rich in such a system become more extensive. Their money gives them power over others, which also infringes the rights of those subservient to them. The rights of consumers bestow upon them improper privileges over other human beings, one of these being institutionalised in the international sex industry.

At every point, there are linkages between the abuses that everyone wants checked and the global integration which allows of no alternative. Global integration leads in so many cases to local disintegration, socially, culturally and psychically. It is partly a willed and wilful unknowing which makes the authorities in the receiving countries treat the women as though they were criminals – imprisoning or deporting them, rather than perceiving them as victims of a slavery which the 'civilised world' prefers to think of as long over and done with: for the violations of human rights are directly traceable to a global market that turns everything it touches to commodity and profit, including the young countrywomen of South Asia, born to vanished subsistence and growing insecurity.

It is not difficult to trace these connections. The commodification of women instantly reduces them to the level of any other item of trade in which they cease to be free. For one thing, women who enter the labour market in this way are not in any sense entering into a contractual relationship. They are without the necessary information with which they could make an informed judgement. They are sold by traffickers to brothel and bar owners and compelled to pay debts which others have incurred in their transfer into the country to which they are traded. They are without legal papers and therefore can be coerced into accepting oppressive working conditions. Their earnings are appropriated by others. They neither fix, nor agree to, the money for which they work.

Occasionally, they are not even permitted to protect themselves against infection by the use of condoms. One young woman spoke of the agony of being expected to have frequent sexual intercourse, even with a condom: the sores and wounds which the friction caused subjected her to continuous pain. Women may be subjected to HIV tests without being informed of the result.

When immigration laws are enforced, women are criminalised by the receiving country, treated as illegal immigrants and deported. When they seek help from police, immigration officials, they are often subjected to further abuse and sexual violence. Their children may be refused the nationality of the country of their birth, as well as the country of origin.

Siriporn Skrobanek, of the Foundation for Women, recommends that trafficked women should not be subject to immigration laws and that they should be entitled to compensation from traffickers. Migrant prostitutes should be considered as undocumented workers and protected by ILO conventions.

Oan (not her real name) was married to a Swiss national. She was used by him to earn money as a sex worker. She managed to get away from Zurich and is now working in Pattaya. She had learned French. She said,

To work freely is one thing, but to work by force for your husband is a form of slavery. I was married to the man who abused me. The clients could see what was happening and to them he made no secret of it. He sold me to them for sex. Some did, but there was one man in particular who was kind to me and who helped me to escape. He paid for my flight back to Bangkok. When I came back, I had to make a living. I had left my two children in Chiang Rai and, during eight years, I could send no money home. My mother was very angry with me and I feel I have to make up to her all the years I was away. She does not know what happened. She thinks I was having a good time in Europe. People think all those who go away are earning a lot of money and she blamed me for not sharing it with her. I could not tell her what I had been through and this makes me very sad. But to be in Pattaya now is to be free. My life is good, but my heart is not happy.

The Foundation for Women has a wide dossier on the fate of women abducted or tricked into prostitution abroad, including a woman who was forced into prostitution in Japan and jumped out of a window to escape the criminal mafia. She was refused treatment by two hospitals and is permanently disabled as a consequence. Three other Thai women who had been held captive in a brothel killed their captor. They were charged with murder, and the prosecutor demanded life imprisonment. The Foundation for Women and other organisations launched an international compaign on their behalf, and finally, they were sentenced to ten years imprisonment. The three women appealed, and the jail terms were reduced to eight years.

It is impossible to exaggerate the violence of these forms of coercive prostitution. A desire for self-improvement, especially of poor rural women, which is fed both by the growing poverty of their home-place and the lure of consumerism, makes them vulnerable to the promises of agents and recruiters; particularly when these are people they know, from their own province or neighbourhood. It is bad enough when traditional cultures are undermined and disparaged by the global media; when the minds and hearts of a young generation are penetrated by fantasies from distant markets, the very purpose of which is the spread of radical dissatisfaction with the local and familiar. Yet all this is felt to be quite normal; the right to self-determination of a human being over her own body and life is in fact only a more tangible and dramatic example of people's loss of control over self-reliance and indigenous values all over the world.

The Asia Rights Watch published its report on trafficking of Burmese women to Thailand in December 1993, *A Modern Form of Slavery*. Thirty girls and women were interviewed in depth and a clear picture emerges of the ruthless efficiency with which around 20,000 Burmese women are recruited and deployed in the Thai sex industry. The women are generally lured by agents who promise legal jobs in Thailand. They are brought to the border, often by unsuspecting relatives, who receive payment – up to 800 dollars, which then becomes the 'debt' of the captive. Any young woman who seeks to leave the brothels risks being arrested – and the police are often major clients of the brothels – or jeopardises the security of her family, who will be pursued for defaulting on the 'debt'. Women work between 10 and 18 hours a day, 25 days a month, with between 5 and 15 clients a day. Many become HIV-positive. They are frequently moved around from brothel to brothel to satisfy the 'need' for new faces.

The accounts given by women who have been traded in this way – those interviewed by the Foundation for Women, the Centre for the Protection of Children's Rights and Asia Rights Watch, among others – suggest they are plunged violently into an incomprehensible world, in which they are disoriented and disadvantaged in every way. Many of the girls and women did not understand what was happening to them until they were compelled to have sex in the brothels. They did not know what was expected of them until those they had trusted as guides and befrienders showed themselves as exploiters. They were brought to cities whose names they did not know, where they could not read the street signs. Many who came to Bangkok could not identify the area where they had lived, rarely went out and, if they did, spoke to no one for fear of being captured or stolen, or of revealing their illegal status. They did not understand how the debts they incurred were assessed, nor how much they earned. Some assumed that their parents had sanctioned the work they were doing and accepted it. They spoke of being given a number and being made to sit in a lighted room, so that they could be selected like merchandise by clients window-shopping. It suggests a world of brutal transitions from village to metropolis, from farming to an industrialised sex trade, traumatic transplanting from paddy fields to prostitution. Many could not speak or understand Thai. They spoke of journeys by car, where they passed checkpoints and frontiers with the connivance of police and officials. Many of their customers were the same people who later raided the brothels, arrested them and then abused them all over again.

In 'AIDS and Prostitution in Thailand, Case Study of Burmese Prostitution in Ranong' (unpublished thesis May 1992), Hnin Hnin Pyne divides the means of entry into prostitution into three broad channels: voluntary, whereby the woman aproaches the sex establishment herself; bonded, whereby parents or guardians take money from an agent or brothel owner; and involuntary, which means the coercion or deception of a woman into prostitution. The latter is by far the most common means for the Burmese women investigated by Asia Rights Watch. Networks are often informal: relatives know of a temple or shop in their area where agents may be contacted. Most were accompanied to the border by a relative, friend or teacher; almost invariably an exchange of money took place (usually around 200 dollars), although the nature of the transaction was unclear to the victim. This became part of the young woman's debt, towards repayment of which her future earnings was pledged in advance. Occasionally girls or young women were abducted even close to their home, while tending buffaloes in the fields or shopping in the market. Many were humiliated, raped or 'tested for virginity' en route, as they passed between a succession of drivers, policemen and agents; and they stayed only a few months in each brothel, before being moved on. Many understood that their share of their own earnings was around one-third; but they rarely saw it and their debt never diminished. Sometimes they were given counters instead of money, the accumulation of which was supposed to enable them to count off the repayment of their debt. In some cases, their only earnings were the scant tips given them by clients over and above the charge levied by the brothel keepers.

Section 34 of the Thai Penal Code explicitly forbids debt bondage, yet nearly all the trafficked women are subject to this form of involuntary labour. For many young women, the idea of 'debt' merged with the less palpable form of obligation which Thai children owe to their parents; and many of them simply decided to work as hard as possible to pay off that measureless duty. Some had excessive numbers of clients in a very short time, many of them soldiers, police and border guards. The young women interviewed by the Asia Rights Watch reported that half had had clients who were policemen. Sometimes, the women recognised clients among those who had come to 'rescue' them during police raids. Most had no communication with their families while held in the brothels. They were not allowed to refuse clients. They had to pay for their own medical care and saw a doctor only when it became essential. Some of the conditions in the brothels were unhygienic and insanitary: the women often worked and lived in cubicles where the beds are only concrete bunks. Most were given contraceptive pills.

The role of the government of Thailand in all this is instructive. Despite publicised 'crackdowns' from time to time, (the Chuan Leek Pai administration announced one in November 1992), the involvement of officials, police, politicians, in trafficking and brothel ownership means that there is little effective action taken. While the traffickers get away with it, the women are arrested as prostitutes or illegal immigrants and are deported, with all that implies of abuse and further violation of rights en route and thence to punitive detention and imprisonment once they are back in Burma. These are indiscriminately 'repatriated' to Burma. If they belong to those regional and ethnic groups groups fighting the government (the Shan, Karen and Mon people in particular) which are in more or less open warfare with the brutal military junta that rules the country, the State Law and Order Restoration Council, their fate is likely to be even worse.

The Asia Rights Watch reports that there is only one case of a brothel owner ever having been punished under the Penal Code: in 1984, a fire broke out in Phuket and five women were burned to death, because they were chained up in the room. Charges were filed against the brothel owners and the case lasted seven years. They were eventually imprisoned and the families of the victims compensated.

In 1985, Thailand ratified the Convention on the Elimination of All Forms of Discrimination Against Women (CEDAW), which pledges to 'take all appropriate measures, including legislation, to modify or abolish existing laws, regulations, customs and practices which constitute discriminationn against women' and to 'accord to women equality with men before the law'. Part of the failure to implement the laws protecting women comes from a deeper cultural ambiguity which sees the sexual appetites of men as natural and necessary, but deplores 'promiscuity' in women and treats it as a phenomenon to be punished and reformed. This is reflected in the discriminatory arrest pattern, even of those women who have been systematically trafficked, abused and violated.

The Thai government is increasingly concerned with 'illegal migrants'. Thailand, as a major regional capital and as a model of 'development' in South Asia, has become the destination of many economic migrants from neighbouring countries. Among the 'illegal workers' in Thailand, there are an estimated

330,000 from Burma, many of them in the sex industry as well as in the construction industry, 100,000 from India and Bangladesh, 100,000 from China (some of these young women trafficked from Yunnan) and about 20,000 from Cambodia and Laos. The movement of peoples set in train by economic development is in reality unstoppable, given the mobility now accorded to goods and money; particularly when there is no limit on the movement of rich people, especially in the form of tourism, now one of the biggest and most lucrative industries in the world. People will keep coming across borders, whether as legal labour to relieve shortages in parts of Thailand or as clandestine immigrants. These, still overwhelmingly male, added to the Thai men who habitually use prostitutes, will ensure that women will continue to be brought – by whatever means – to Thailand to service them and to create fortunes for those who traffic, control and manipulate them.

II

September 1995. The area is badly affected by floodwater. A monotonous urban landscape, a long straight road, visibility impaired by a bluish haze from trapped car fumes; low-rise buildings from the 1960s, flat and featureless, relieved only by an occasional gilt and brightly painted temple; footbridges across the otherwise impassable roads. Outside the Foundation for Women building there is a tree: the only growing thing in the street, a mass of yellow blossoms that merge into a single golden haze; a reproach to the urban environment and a triumphant assertion of life. Siriporn Skrobanek of the Foundation of Women had just returned from Beijing, where she had addressed the NGO Forum on trafficking in women.

This has become a more and more lucrative trade. In Japan, they can make 400,000 baht from one woman (15,000 US dollars). A recent case revealed that ten women had netted four million baht for the traffickers.

Labour is seen as an export commodity. The only legal employment for women abroad is as domestic labour and we saw what can happen to them in the case of the 16-year-old girl in the United Arab Emirates, recently sentenced to death for killing an employer who raped her. She was later reprieved and her sentence reduced.

To go abroad as a sex worker is forbidden; even where prostitution is legal, you cannot go and work in those countries. It is the illegality of their position that keeps women under the control of the traffickers. Even if they get 40 per cent of what they earn, they will tolerate that because it is more than they would get in their home country. In Japan, we know of women who receive nothing. They are, in effect, bonded labour; and that is Japan – the country that is supposed to be an economic inspiration to the rest of the world.

The victims of trafficking are getting younger. In the 1980s, agents went to recruit those already in the sex industry, young women over 20. Now they go to the villages to find pupils, teenagers. They find plenty: here, in Thailand, their childhood has already been stolen by work.

There are sophisticated networks of traffickers, but their methods are crude. Everybody would like to migrate because of the money. Some of the women pay middlemen to facilitate migration. Many know exactly what they will do if they go to Japan; what they do not know are the conditions and the exploitation they will suffer. They do not know that the money will not be theirs, that they are merely objects in a transaction, not employees in any normal sense of the word. We are asking for a wider definition of trafficking than that which exists now, to include recruitment both by deception and by force.

There is already a strong tradition of migration from the north of Thailand; by tradition, I mean it has been established some 40 years or so. It is part of a strategy for household survival that makes people migrate. International migration is a newer phenomenon. Government has a labour export policy, but only to earn money for Thailand, not to protect the workers. There is no control of labour export agencies, even though migration is itself encouraged. Labour is seen as an abstraction, not as flesh and blood.

Of course, the well-educated have always migrated. Doctors go to the USA. People with academic qualifications will go to the West, those with professional skills will go to where they can command a higher price. No one stops them – they can look after themselves and add to the wealth of the receiving country.

This same attitude is extended to women who go to do other work, in the entertainment or prostitution industries. It is of no concern to the Thai authorities, even though it may be to the authorities of the receiving countries. They say they cannot intervene. What we say is that people are free only if they make well-informed decisions. Our strategy is to provide information to people, not just the one-sided information of the recruiters.

What we are talking about is campaigns against slavery. Traffickers are mostly male, although some women are involved. Even women already in prostitution in Bangkok want to work overseas. They do not know the tricks of traffickers. Promises are falsely given to village families – that their daughters are going to Germany to work in the fields, to pick apples, to pick strawberries. They believe it and by the time they discover the truth it is too late.

Trafficking in Thailand is changing. More and more children are going to secondary school. People in the villages now know where to go if they want to work in the sex industry. This is why traffickers turn to Burmese girls and the ethnic minorities, as well as girls from China. Thai women are still enticed to go outside of Thailand – this is a more sophisticated kind of trickery, so the older tricks are now played on those who are more naive.

Many of the trafficked women finish up locked into the low-class brothels. There are many in Bangkok. The Health Office makes no arrests, but it does conduct medical check-ups. The women are controlled, but they do not get access to the medical and social services they need. It is even worse when there is a government crackdown on brothels or karaoke lounges. Repression leads to concealment – this is what happened under the Chuan Leek Pai government. Under the guise of AIDS prevention, the sex trade goes underground and becomes even harder to reach.

The problems are constantly shifting, both in response to the market and to official policies. The abduction of children is a serious issue. There have been a number of stories in the newspapers of children abducted from schools. Therefore, children need protection; but the children of the poor – who will protect them?

In the Netherlands, the Foundation Against Trafficking gets support from the government. We would not want to lose our autonomy by being government-supported. In any *case, the government is not sympathetic. In Beijing they were annoyed with the NGOs who said there are 150,000 to 200,000 prostitutes in Thailand. The government sent a letter saying there are only 70,000 to 80,000. They do not want to acknowledge the extent of the industry, let alone of the trafficking.*

The Police Department is implicated in the control of the rackets; the police in other countries too. Even in Japan, the authorities are involved at every level. There, women in prison are sexually harassed. Some are told they have to provide sex for the police. Supply and demand are interconnected, of course. The development model is also pushing people to need and to want more. It sows dissatisfaction in people's lives. The only way for the poor to attain some of the things they want is to sell their labour, their body, even sometimes, their children.

All this is in addition to the transfer of the Thai patron-client relationship on to trafficking. The families of the trafficked women often feel gratitude to those who will buy their daughters. If the daughter changes from being a victim into a survivor, she will give her parents an income, she will improve their house; and people will accept. This feeds trafficking also: people will not take action against those who violate their rights and a collusive relationship is set up. We see a distortion of the patron-client relationship, which has been reshaped by the modern world. This form of violation of rights, which people acquiesce in, because they see it as a form of survival, is very difficult. It is a cultural problem and hence there is limited role for the law in suppressing it. The legal framework is simply alien to this relationship. Relationships that are spiritual, emotional, psychological, escape legal sanction. It is a long-term issue, not merely a local problem: the whole official apparatus of indifference and laissez-faire must be taken on. You cannot stop people from wanting more, from being prepared to pay more money for virgins from Burma or Yunnan. This echoes the argument now deployed by sex tourists, who say they are doing good to the poor, helping some impoverished family: this is intended to make sex tourism appear as though it were a refinement of development aid.

In Beijing, the NGO Forum brought out some interesting

differences between women's groups. The abolitionist view *[of prostitution]* is, we feel, not in accordance with the present situation. While we have to bring protection and assistance to the victims of international trafficking, we have to take into consideration the basic rights of adult women in prostitution as well. We see that repressive measures against prostitution are not helpful to women; these merely disperse the industry and drive it underground. To empower women and give them rights is not to make a moral judgement. Privileged women cannot speak for sex workers. The best we can do is facilitate their voices.

There was a strong abolitionist movement in Beijing. This reflects, in a way, the haves against the have-nots, a kind of class antagonism. The abolitionists are, on the whole, privileged. They are class-based fundamentalists. Some said I was an instrument of the West. It is so patronising: because my country is a centre for prostitution and trafficking, my concern for the women was interpreted as condoning it and the conclusion was therefore that I must be in collusion with the traffickers!

We must not fight with the abolitionists. The 1949 Convention on Traffic in Persons needs to be reviewed because, I believe, it is not relevant to the phenomenon of today. Yet the abolitionists also want to reinforce the 1949 Convention, to eliminate all forms of sexual exploitation, including female infanticide, wife beating, dowry death, prostitution, traffic in women in general; but their main target remains prostitution. The main thing, in my view, is crimes against humanity and those must be our target. In one workshop in Beijing, a sex worker, a Latin American woman, challenged the abolitionists. She said 'You say you are speaking for me, but you are against me. How can this be?'

Perhaps the most effective way to reduce sex tourism would be to make Thai prostitutes more professional, more like their counterparts in the West, so that they perform their job more mechanistically, without any frills or feelings, with no display of emotion. They should also become more expensive. Then it will stop. Men will stop coming if they find the sex workers here have the same attitude as those in their own countries and charge the same high prices.

9

CHILDREN'S RIGHTS
IN THAILAND

I

In any discussion of the intensely charged expressions 'pedophilia' or 'child prostitution', it is necessary to define what is meant by pedophilia and by childhood.

If pedophilia refers to sex with pre-pubertal children, then it almost certainly concerns a very small minority of sex tourists. In Thailand, for the most part, it is, as Sanphosit of the Center for the Protection of Children's Rights says, 'often confined within families, especially stepfathers and stepbrothers, or neighbours and family friends'. This is not to minimise the particular ugliness of those foreigners who go to Thailand, the Philippines or Sri Lanka or indeed, anywhere else, where they feel that sex with small children is either 'more acceptable', or where they feel they can get away with it because of the 'innocence' of the culture (another racist projection), or where philanthropy (the giving of money, whether to the child or her family) may serve as a cloak for abuse. And the prosecution of Western offenders in their own countries is now widely recognised as a deterrent in most European countries, Australia and the USA. Although Britain has lagged behind its European neighbours on this, a Home Office Review in July 1996 on extra-territorial jurisdiction announced the adoption of a set of policy guidelines agianst which proposals for taking extra-territorial jurisdiction over individual offences committed abroad by British citizens and residents should be judged. The Home

Secretary stated: 'The Review further advises that sexual offences committed against children abroad satisfied a number of criteria in the guidelines and, in the light of that, we have decided that we should take extra-territorial jurisdiction over such offences.'

If the term 'child' refers to those between the ages of 12 and 16 – or even 18 – then it is clear that the problem is far more widespread, and enforcement becomes correspondingly both more difficult and would require a level of policing which it is, at present, hard to conceive. Even in Patpong, in the more open, international part of the sex trade, teenagers – both boys and girls – are highly conspicuous, both in bars and on the streets. Bangkok, like many cities in South Asia, has under-age sex workers who work the shopping malls, the hotels and the streets. The most effective means of rescuing them – as indeed, their Western counterparts in the amusement arcades, streets and clubs of the West – would be a form of economic development that does not lead to growing inequality, more and more exclusion and marginalisation of the poorest. Since this is not on offer even in the West, it is unreasonable to expect it to be so in those countries which have accepted the economic model proposed for the world by Western interests. Having said that, there are elements in Thai history and culture which go some way to explain why Thailand should have become a focus for child prostitution.

One significant traditional aspect of Thai culture has been to regard subordinates as property. During wars and conflicts in this region of Southeast Asia, the victors did not overrun the land of those they had conquered: rather they captured the people and took them to their own territory, so that they would become integrated as part of the productive capacity of the victors. Similarly, peasants were the property of feudal lords who were themselves subordinated to the power of kings. The family became a microcosm of feudal society, wherein the powerlessness of the head of family in the wider world became total power within the more limited domain of the family.

The selling of children was commonplace until the reforms that began only in the mid-nineteenth century. Wives and children were held responsible for crimes committed by the head of the family: there was little sense that they had a separate identity. The relationship was one of institutionalised servitude. Absolute parental power was vested in the father. There was no provision in traditional law for defining limits on the exercise of this power, which clearly provided all kinds of possibilities for exploitation and abuse of children. In 1865, the king, Rama IV, declared that the selling of children as slaves to work for others was unfair. 'Children should not be sold without consent of their own.' This pronouncement – which had the effect of becoming law – was made in response to a case brought before the king. It was then stated that children could be sold only with their consent and should agree to the price, so that the child could later redeem her or his status at that same price.

This was the first step towards legal emancipation. In spite of this, custom and practice are not necessarily changed by edict. Parental power, in all other respects, remained absolute; and the law was slow to forbid explicitly unreasonable punishment or murder of a child.

The enactment of the Criminal Code in 1908 ended slavery completely. Since the buying and selling of adults was prohibited, it also became a crime to buy and sell children. But ancient practices are not so easily eradicated. They have a way of adapting to circumstances and finding other ways into a culture that is changing. Traditions live on in other guises. For instance, a child could still be offered as a gift to a debtor, by way of cancellation; a girl could be offered as debt payment and she would become the mistress of the creditor, since this was not expressly forbidden. Later, even when the Civil and Commercial Code was enacted and the trading in persons was outlawed, ways around the commerce in children were found – unofficial sexual bondage or children given as labour on the land of others, ensured that traditions were perpetuated, even though the starkness of the older practice may have been somewhat muted.

The rights and duties of children remained under parental control until 1934; by which time parental punishment was circumscribed. The law merely stated that such punishment must be carried out 'in a reasonable manner'. The child could file a petition for the court to withdraw parental power, if it were not exercised in good faith. However, this changed little, except in cases where the child was so visibly damaged that its treatment at the hands of a father attracted public attention, which in turn demanded the intervention of the court.

The ideology of patriarchal power in Thailand is the distant inheritor of Chinese and Indian cultures, which make parents not merely the begetters of the child but also the controllers of her or his destiny. Duties of children to parents are enshrined in customary and traditional law and punishments for the infringement of these are draconian.

One consequence of this has been that as Thailand has become industrialised, family laws remain, often unspoken yet widely understood, because they are part of a shared culture; and the state has been slow to intervene in the power of the family (the father) over its members, even on behalf of the rights of children. The family enjoys an autonomy and independence, which have only recently come to be questioned. Of course, parents have responsibility for the protection and care of the child until she is able to look after herself and if they fail to do so, social disapproval is certain; but there are no legal sanctions against such failure. Public condemnation of children failing in their duties is far more likely to be both vocal and shaming. The moral disciplines (dhamma) of Buddhism enjoin upon children the duty to support their parents, work for them, maintain the family traditions, become worthy of their heritage and make offerings for their parents' merit. In return, parents are supposed to keep children from evil, train them to virtue, arrange their marriages and hand over their inheritance when the time comes.

The Centre for the Protection of Children's Rights (CPCR) has been one of the principal NGOs in Thailand working towards a more equitable distribution of family duties and responsibilities than that enshrined in custom and practice. They argue that conservative practice is at odds with contemporary society: increased mobility, migration, the decay of traditional village cultures, urbanisation, industrialisation, have led to significant shifts in sensibility. These things sometimes become the conduits through which the older traditions survive; thus, child labour, prostitution, and exploitative labour can all be interpreted as means of expressing the measureless duties of children to parents. Indeed, the extraordinary endurance and capacity for sustaining relentless hours of work among young women in the garment industry, as well as the rigours accepted by sex workers, can often be traced to this sense of duty. It can easily be seen how this clashes with the perceptions of Westerners.

Although the Civil and Commercial Code provides a court with the authority to withdraw parental power from those who abuse their children's rights, it is a complicated procedure which serves to deter most victims from using it: only the child's relatives or the Public Prosecutor can apply to the court for the revocation of parental rights. This in itself makes it unlikely to occur, except in extreme cases. Protection of children can only begin after an offence has been committed – such as when a child has already been sold into prostitution or exploitative labour. During such proceedings, the child is expected to remain in the power of the parents. A child has the right to enter civil or criminal actions against her or his parents, but only on application to the court by herself or her close relatives. CPCR has seen only two or three cases – out of hundreds – that have been initiated by relatives. Those referred to the Public Prosecutor tend to be very extreme – murder or assaults, or abuse that inflict terrible injuries.

CPCR attributes the problem with the law to the fact that much of Thai law has been adopted from the European tradition and has not emerged out of the living tissue of Thai society and norms, with the result that the theory is at odds with the reality: the law permits the state to intervene before a crime has been committed, but there is no means whereby the Public Prosecutor can possibly learn of the anticipated crime; similarly, even when there has been some crime, it is extremely difficult for the agencies of the state to intervene in the private, even secretive, life of the family. Unless state officers are given authority to take immediate action, they are powerless to prevent abuse, exploitation or parental connivance in children entering a life of exploited labour or going into the sex industry.

The law against sexual offences reserves the heaviest penalties for acts of 'rape and copulation' which may result in pregnancy. This omits offences against younger girls and assumes that boys are not subject to sexual assault. The Labour Act protects child labour in so far as conditions of employment go, but does not extend to forced labour which is detrimental to the child's well-being. Since most child labourers reside with the employer, who assumes the equivalent of parental power over the child, this power can then be used to extract maximum labour from the child. Indeed, this may be one reason why labour has been notably tractable and docile in the industrial sector in Thailand. In particular in the garments industry, where tens of thousands of young women live in the small row-house factories, they regard their employers as givers of work, who feed and house them, rather than as makers of profit: the extension of the parental model is a powerful force for acceptance. This may also be true to some extent in the sex industry; but even where young women are well aware of their captivity and loathe their captors, it is likely that in the end their duty to parents reconciles many of them, to some degree, even to these conditions of abusive wretchedness.

II

Sudarat Srisang has been one of the pioneers in the movement against child prostitution in Thailand. She has now left ECPAT and has been instrumental in the formation of FACE, the Fight Against Child Exploitation. We met at Rangsit University, an open campus far out of the centre of Bangkok, beyond the airport. We sat in a seminar room, overlooking rainswept grass and rectangular faculty buildings, while Sudarat expressed her outrage at the assault upon the children of her country.

The demand for younger women is increasing in the sex industry. When people want to avoid AIDS, they want fresh, unspoilt girls or children. Normal people do not want sex with children. Most sex tourists, of course, are not pedophiles. Since 1982, we know of organised sex tours from Holland, Germany, the USA, the UK, Switzerland, but not for sex with minors. Now there are entrepreneurs who are arranging excursions specially for those who want children.

ECPAT was formed in late 1987. We have been monitoring the impact of change upon social and cultural habits in Thailand. Since 1982 I have studied prostitution, both in Thailand and in Europe. I did not think of child prostitution at that time. There had been a few cases, but we did not think this was of central importance. We thought tourism produced beggar chil-

dren, which it does; but as we came
ised that they were selling their bodies to

The odd cases we were aware of w
from Hong Kong or Singapore and one or t
know that some Chinese have strange ideas a
believe in aphrodisiacs, bear paws or monke
increase potency. There is also a belief that having
virgins, or with young girls who have not menstrua
supposed to prolong life and provide energy. These
archaic cultural practices; but we did not think that suc
people who came as tourists would seek sex with children.
We were looking at some other link; we knew tourism had a
negative impact on children, but we did not know that Thailand, together with the Philippines and Sri Lanka, is the
biggest provider of child prostitutes.

In Pattaya and Chiang Mai, local people as well as
foreigners use prostitutes. There are older women as well as
young girls under 15; we found some of these in bars, doing
striptease. They were available to locals and foreigners, whoever wanted to take them off from the bar.

By 1990, foreign use – or rather, abuse – of children was
increasing and receiving big publicity. School pupils were
arrested by the Ministry of Education, a number of truants
were found in the Suriwong Hotel. Since then, news of such
things has become common. At the very time when we took
up the issue, in 1989, there was the case of an American,
working as a boys' guardian, semi-officially, who was systematically abusing the street children he was suppposed to be
helping. Similar stories have come from India, Cambodia –
men trusted by the community to look after delinquent or
abandoned boys, who use them for sexual purposes.

In the 1980s, some parents in the North were accused of
selling their children to work as child labour in factories.
They were sending money home and it was a source of pride
to the parents that they were helping to support the family.
It was not their intention to sell their children. Today, there
are stories of parents selling children into prostitution. There
are a few, but it is very rare; most are deceived, imagining
their children are going to work in a hotel or shop rather
than a brothel.

We are seeing a decline of ethical values in society: this is

values of the people. The
child prostitution as a Thai
he suppliers. It is not only
cus of concern.
my husband went to a
as a Vital Force for Peace.
e was reported back to the
is in Canada for defaming
by the police in Thailand.
rism, we will arrest, it is
oke out against tourism at
thought to be dangerous
ator of income.

TS IN THAILAND

151

to know them, we real-
re Chinese people
o Japanese. We
out sex, they
brains to
sex with
ted, is

..., together with our friends in the West, should do whatever we can to raise awareness of the sexploitation of children. Of course, many benefit from it. Even teachers here sometimes deceive and recruit children, as has also happened in Taiwan. Doctors are sometimes implicated as well, those who repair the vagina of an abused girl or attend to other injuries. There are lawyers, too, who help the brothel owners, so a whole network of professionals have a vested interest in it, together with the customers who, naturally, are going to remain silent.

Demand as well as supply: traffic in children is now considerable, from Yunnan in China, Burma, Laos. They are advertised in Singapore, Hong Kong. Older women – I mean 19- or 20-year-olds – are going into international prostitution in Europe. Many women here think of the sex tourist as a man on a white horse, the rich farang who will rescue them and set them up in Europe. So they make a relationship. She thinks, 'This farang loves me.' She decides to marry him, to live abroad, become a housewife, forget her past. A few get good husbands, but most do not. Either the man becomes the pimp in Frankfurt or wherever, or he will make her work for him. The men may have borrowed money to come to Thailand. One woman we knew went to work packing apples for one of them. She saw him as rich, he saw her as caring. There was no real relationship and absolutely no understanding: a scenario for disaster.

The whole conception of tourism is Western. We do not have tourism as a cultural activity. We do not have long *holidays – the Chinese New Year maybe, but we work and relax, work and relax – it is a different rhythm from the holidays of four to six weeks which Europeans expect. In fact, industrial society gives people the idea that they have a right to do anything. They believe they have a right to spend, especially when they go somewhere else where all the social constraints are in abeyance. You see people dressed for the beach walking in Bangkok. It does not matter what you do on vacation in the 'Somewhere Else', it doesn't matter how badly you treat the people, how you violate their customs and social values. This is the malignancy of tourism. And when anything goes, it is not long before even the most vulnerable, the children, fall victim to the strange tastes that arise from this urge to try something new, taste the exotic. It is, above all, racist. Away from home, they are not Mr X or Mr Y, they won't be judged. At home, they may be a teacher, a professor, something respectable; but in a strange land, they can do anything, no one will know.*

We work with the Tourist Authority of Thailand to control, not to promote, tourism. It is no use just measuring the numbers who come or the sum of money they bring. You have to count the social costs, not merely the income generated. Only by seeing the wider context can you measure whether or not it is beneficial to Thailand.

We have formed FACE, a task force to fight child exploitation, with an advisory board including the Attorney-General, the Deputy Commander of the Crime Suppression Division and a Permanent Secretary from the Prime Minister's Office. We produce pamphlets for foreigners, telling them of penalties for crimes committed against children under 15. Of course, not all such people are pedophiles – they might go to a bar and if some young person makes them an offer, they just give in.

The problem lies with the developmental model we are following and the belief that there is no alternative to it. When we were younger, we went to a Karen village on the Burmese border, because we were very romantic about the simple life. There was no rice mill and the women had to spend the whole morning pounding. The roof of grass was cool, but it had to be renewed annually and with such labour. We had to shut our mouth about the ideal peaceful life. We went with the women to fetch water, which was their burden. Who would not want tap water? How could we tell them not to imitate the rich, not to want tap water and electricity? It is such a hard life.

But there must be another kind of development between the constant hard labour of the village and the raging consumerism of the West. Of course, women are now used as an excuse for the excesses of consumerism – it lightens their burden, therefore it must be good, no matter what denatured stuff comes in our foods, no matter what dangerous chemicals feed the crops.

Buddhism tells us to limit our needs. But the people have no power to define their needs – they don't need prostitution or a 12-hour day in a factory. These things are phenomena of an unjust society. In many Third World countries, people are happier when they can work in a subsistence economy. When the change comes to a market-oriented economy, they are lost. But it is government policy to encourage the market. The industrial sector has become powerful and demands a reduction of tax on industry, so the agricultural sector is neglected. Farmers collapse, become migrants, construction workers, labourers. Families are broken, husbands and wives separate and this creates serious psychological disturbance for children. If the government paid more attention to agricultural life, people would be happier than working in a factory far from their family. Farmers used to grow vegetables, shrimps and fish – all destroyed by pollutants. They cannot survive. They become poor where there was plenty and they must migrate.

Tourism is seen as a way of getting the money to pay off the country's debt to the IMF and the World Bank. They have to build bigger hotels, better roads, more resorts, to attract foreigners. In Kenya, for every dollar earned by the tourist industry, 1.50 dollars has to be spent on foreign contractors, consultants, buying in all the luxuries that foreign tourists want. It turns out to be a drain on the resources of the country, not a gain; and when you add the social costs, it becomes disastrous. Tourists are not going to pay for the health care of sex workers with AIDS.

Soon after we started ECPAT, it became an international campaign. Taiwan is both receiving pedophiles from Thailand

and sending them here. Vietnam and Cambodia are also becoming centres for such activity. At the government level, the laws have to be both amended and enforced. Germany, Sweden, Australia and the US now have laws which can punish in their own country any of their nationals who commit offences against children abroad. We are now trying to get the West to change its law on child pornography. I have had some discussion with Sanphosit of the Centre for the Protection of Children's Rights. He says that such open campaigns drive it underground. I think this is better than permitting it to be visible, letting it happen. It is wrong to allow children to be like food at a table, let the customers choose. At least this way, society can signal its disapproval.

We have to raise awareness, awareness as a preliminary to action. We must get the public to inform on brothels, the secret places where the girls are kept. Boys are not kept in closed brothels. Girls are hidden, boys are on the streets.

More children are running away from home. The mother gets married again or takes in a boyfriend when her husband has gone to work as a migrant labourer. He drinks and beats the child. A boy will run away, sleep in a lodging house, take a shower in the canal. If a man comes along and offers him a shower in an apartment, gives him new clothes, food, he will accept. But once he has been used sexually, he may start to wander, go from man to man. Some children won't testify. There is one boy, now 20, who was used by an American when he was 14. This man was arrested, but the boy still wants to go and live with his molester in the United States. On the other hand, the boy molested by the Swede Bengt Bolin did not like it, he was forced by the man. There was a case of a German, who had taken some 12- and 13- year-olds. He gave them food and toys. He didn't use them sexually, but told them to do it with each other. This was to advertise sex tours, part of a marketing technique. Most girls are locked away and this is worse. We found one who had been brought by her grandmother to Patpong. Some are brought by parents to hotels where they are offered to foreigners.

Abused children become abusers. One 17-year-old was taken by a man to Indonesia. When he came back, he had sex with a 12-year-old in Pattaya, whom he then killed. To deal with the abuser is not the end. He must be punished for the sake of justice to the children. Bengt Bolin (a Swedish national who was tried and found guilty in Sweden for crimes committed against children in Southeast Asia) was also required to pay compensation. He was made an example to any of his fellow-countrymen who might have been contemplating such a trip. In addition, we have to work with the family, to heal the situation.

It is all very well to legislate against abuse of children, but the policy adopted by the government tends towards the splitting of families, migration and break-up. Development, consumerism, the desire for goods – people are driven to desperate methods to achieve them; for this, some will even sell their own children. This shows what a distorted, unnatural development this is.

III

It would be quite wrong to imagine that Thailand depends upon Western campaigns to fight for the rights of children. The Centre for the Protection of Children's Rights (CPCR) has taken a lead in the effort to gain recognition for wrongs committed against children, both by Western visitors and by Thais. Although sex tourism which has as its object the children of South Asia (or indeed, Central or South America or Africa) has its origins among the well-to-do travellers, the West does not have a monopoly of abusers: there are many in the receiving countries themselves; and Sanphosit, Director of CPCR, recognises that while child sex tourism is a particular evil, it is essentially the money power of the rich visitors which distinguishes them from child abusers in Thailand. He also insists that abuse has many guises; and the concern with sexual abuse should not eclipse other assaults, physical and emotional, which also injure and impair the lives of children.

The Centre is in a drab suburb of East Bangkok, an area developed in the 1960s, with three- or four-storey buildings with monotonous concrete arcades at roof level; a place of dusty flyovers, 7–11 shops, food vendors with wooden carts and metal and glass display cases of roast duck, chicken, papaya salad, vats of tomyam over a gas ring connected to a cylinder. There are derelict buildings in course of demolition, rusty metal security grilles and heavy concrete rubble. Lengths of corrugated tin shield construction sites colonised by coarse grass and plantain. Over the desolate landscape towers a shopping mall and the glass and marble showrooms of Mercedes or Volvo. The Centre is away from the main road, close to a temple, with wood-built quarters for the monks adjacent to it, where saffron robes flutter in the breeze. It is actually one of a row of shops and office buildings, with a glass front; outside, a jumble of the shoes of workers and visitors.

CPCR was established 15 years ago. It pioneered the work of child protection, taking up issues that were either not addressed previously or which have only recently emerged with the development of the country. Its purpose is not to do charitable work, but to investigate abuses of the rights of children, to rescue and rehabilitate children whose rights have been infringed and to undertake work of prevention. It conducts campaigns to change legislation, to raise public awareness, both within Thailand and internationally. In the beginning, the issues were child labour and cruelty to children. Over the past decade, emphasis has shifted towards sexual abuse and trafficking in children, including child prostitution.

There are six teams. These are concerned with child advocacy, rescue and rehabilitation, public education, prevention and international relations. Increasingly, the latter deals with the growing number of foreign journalists, teachers and NGOs, who come to learn from the example of the CPCR and to report on its achievements of the past 15 years. The Centre now employs 40 people. In 1996, it plans to register as an independent foundation.

Naw Daisy Saw Aung works with the international relations team. A young woman of Burmese origin, her family was forcibly returned to Burma. She knows her father is dead, but has had no news of the rest of the family for many years. Her early education was in refugee camps, where she learnt English – mainly from volunteers. Her own experience has left her with an insight into, and a sympathy with, the scarrings of dispossessed and abused young people. To be a refugee, to have been effectively orphaned by political upheaval, is itself a profound violation of the rights of children. Daisy says that the issue of child labour remains important. The staff still go into factories to secure the release of child workers. But child sexual abuse, both by Thais and by foreigners, has now become the most pressing concern.

We spoke with Wassana Kaonoparat, lawyer and head of the Rescue and Assistance Team. She came to work here as soon as she finished her studies five years ago.

We work co-operatively with that section of the police which is concerned with child prostitution. The children are in brothels and tea houses, from which many of them rarely go out. We rely on the public to inform us. If someone calls us or writes with the details of some case, we ask the staff to check out if it is true and to try to secure some picture or document that will corroborate the story. This can be a delicate operation, because the owners scarcely welcome intervention. Then we contact the Crime Suppression Division. This is also delicate, because there is a certain amount of collusion between the brothel owners and parts of the Crime Suppression Division. We know who the best people are and we go to them. We soon learn if they are trustworthy.

Sometimes a man will call us who has visited a place for the purpose of prostitution. He may have gone there and found that children are employed. He may contact us or he may simply have confided in a friend, who will then telephone or write to us. We ask for details, we do not accept anonymous calls. Informants must identify themselves; we are not the secret police. Occasionally, you may get people who misinform because they want to get some enemy into trouble or they want revenge against someone. We have an instinct for when we are on a genuine case, but we have to follow it up carefully. We have volunteers who can go and find out the truth. They go to the brothel as potential customers and look round; of course, they don't have sex. Then they report back to us.

We have good volunteers in the north of Thailand. Some of our best informants come from there. There has been a long history of girls being recruited for work in restaurants and hotels and then being taken to brothels, where they are often locked up. Not kidnapped – they go in good faith, they want to work. Some parents do sell their daughters, but although this makes news, it is rare. We have known examples of a father using his own daughter for prostitution from his own house.

We came to know of one Thai girl who had been adopted by Germans, but they did so in order to use her for sexual purposes.

Since 1991, we have been helping Chinese girls from Yunnan. In February 1996, we took four Chinese girls home. We have good relations with the Chinese authorities. On one occasion, we helped 50 girls, aged between 13 and 27, all of them imprisoned in brothels. They come here as illegals and, because of that, they cannot go out: they are told that if they're discovered, they will be jailed. Sometimes, they get no money for their services. The 'owner' buys them through agents, gangs from China. One man will bring a girl and receive money for her and the man who 'buys' her brings her from China into Chiang Rai province near the border.

One group we rescued had walked for ten days in the forest to avoid the checkpoints. Some got sick with malaria. The Chinese authorities have learned in recent years and now they co-operate with us. They are now trying to prevent their young women from leaving the country, showing movies in the villages about what may happen if they go illegally for work. China is quite serious about the border.

Daisy says this is in contrast with Burma. 'You cannot work with the Burmese authorities as you can with the Chinese. Many of the prostitutes we see are Burmese, perhaps the majority. They cannot go home. If they are known to have been prostitutes in Thailand, they will be imprisoned, even executed.' She says there is a brisk commerce in the ID cards of dead Thais, as a response to the illegal status of many migrants. There are many people close to the border, people of mixed race – part Thai, Karen, hill tribes – who cannot get an ID card.

A recent case we are working on is that of a monk, Phavana Phuto. He raped many girls from the hill tribes. He went to a village near Mae Hong Son, where the people are very poor and where the girls desperately wanted to go to school. The monk set up a school, with a hostel for 20 or 30 girls. Under the pretence of doing good work, he was abusing them, girls aged from 10 to 18. The case is being prepared. The girls cannot go home, because if they do, the monk's lawyers will offer them

*and their families money not to testify. We are keeping them
in one of the rehabilitation houses until the trial.*

The rehabilitation houses are for longer-term healing of abused
children. What CPCR really needs, says Sanphosit, their director, is a separate house, a safe house, where those involved in
court cases can remain, a refuge where they will not be threatened or intimidated from giving evidence.

As we sit in the reception area of the Centre, two of the
girls involved in the Phavana Phuto case come in. They are
about 16 or 17, smiling young women in flip-flop sandals
and blue jeans. They are doing some work for the Centre,
pending the trial: newspaper cuttings, which the workers at
the Centre mark for clipping. CPCR is one of the few children's organisations that is empowered to prosecute abusers.

Wassana says that by no means all of the child abuse
cases coming to the Centre involve foreigners. Mostly Thai,
they are more often than not family, neighbours or friends of
the children they molest. But there are also foreigners: when
I visited last year, there was a 15-year-old in the office. He
had been adopted by a family who later had a child of their
own. They then rejected him. He roamed the streets and by
the age of 13, he had fallen into prostitution. He had been
picked up by a Frenchman whose camera he stole. The tourist – foolishly – complained to the police. The camera was
recovered, but the police saw that the film in it consisted
mainly of pornographic pictures of the boy. The Frenchman
was arrested.

*We have only just started serious involvement with foreign
pedophiles. We work closely with ECPAT (End Child Prostitution in Asian Tourism). They pass on information to us.
We don't pursue every case, but we try to concentrate on
those that are most serious and those where we have most
evidence. Then we prepare cases for prosecution where it is
appropriate. We have a case of a pedophile abusing boys in
Phuket. Another foreigner who was living there informed us
about it. We worked closely with the informant and gained a
lot of details. The staff went to investigate and they saw the
children. They were not actually Thai children, so there was
a language problem. The abuser was also a teacher. He was*

taking children on trips to the islands and into the jungle, where he was abusing them.

We have one case concerning a foreigner at the moment; this may lead us to trace the organisation of pedophile groups. If you are a pedophile and you come to Bangkok, you must have contact with someone if you want sex. You cannot easily do it acting alone. Sometimes they make contact through the Internet. They may actually travel alone, but they depend on information from others, networks and groups in foreign countries who will lead them to what they are looking for.

One girl we helped was from Burma. She was working in a restaurant there near the border and wanted to come to Thailand for work. A woman came and asked her if she wanted to work in a restaurant in Bangkok. She said yes. The woman rented a car and it passed through the checkpoint without stopping – she was working with the police. The girl was taken to Chiang Mai, where they spoke to her in Thai, which she could not understand. She was taken to a brothel, where the pimp gave money to the woman who had delivered her. She was taken to a room and only then did she realise she was to work as a prostitute. The pimp told her her debt was 20,000 baht (about 800 US dollars), which she now had to pay back. She had to get new clothes, so the debt increased. She was forced to work till she had paid it all back, as well as the interest. The customers in the brothel are given a price tag and the woman has to collect the tag instead of money. Only half of what was paid was regarded as contributing towards the debt payment of the girl. Through CPCR the brothel was raided: a number of women were being held there, not permitted to go out. That girl is now about 17.

Wassana is called away to the telephone. When she comes back, she says the call was from a man who is separated from his wife. The daughter is with her mother, but he says she is not being allowed to go to school. He wants care of her. His wife used to be a prostitute, an uneducated woman, who had a daughter before he married her.

Most of the work we do is with the children of the poor. Of course, there are problems with rich families as well. Sometimes, the parents buy a condo for their children where they are allowed to stay. The girl or boy calls their friends and they may do bad things, get into trouble. The problems with the higher-status families tend to be more emotional. One woman called because her nephew, who was 14, was having a sexual relationship with a neighbour. The parents didn't agree to it; so the boy and the woman went away together. They say they love each other. In such cases, there is little we can do.

There is often collusion between the young girls and their customers, especially when the girls reach the age of 14 or 15 and it is less obvious that they are minors. We helped one younger girl who was working in Patpong. She had had sex with an Australian. He took her picture and, in the shop where the film was developed, the shopworkers saw the picture. The owner sent it to CPCR. The picture was of a girl with a statue of the Buddha in her vagina. We contacted the Tourist Police and after about ten days, they picked her up in Patpong. She was interviewed and they asked her where this man was. She and her sister, aged 12 and 8, were taken into care. They had been brought by the mother and grandmother and sold to for-eigners. The man's face was also in the picture. It was circulated and, after a week, he was identified by a shop-keeper in Chiang Mai. It was the same man. We helped the 8-year-old, who came to our rehabilitation centre. She said she wanted to study in school. But she didn't really want to. She left. She still calls us and says, 'I want to learn.' She is 14 now and staying with her lover, who is a university student. But we see her sometimes in Patpong. You cannot compel them to be rehabilitated.

We come to hear of many pedophile cases. Most of our callers want to tell us of abuse. This is the main problem now, mostly girls, abused by a father, a stepfather, a relative. We cannot take them all to court; each case requires a lot of study and checking beforehand; the girl must be taken from the home; a psychologist and social worker must then work with the family to see if there is any possibility of reuniting her with them or not.

Rescue is only the beginning. There is much to be done. We co-operate with the Public Prosecutor; but what we really need is a house for the rescue team, a place that can remain secret, so that witnesses are secure and no one can

*reach those who are in danger. At present, we have to find
temporary homes for them.*

Chris Macmahon is an Australian working at CPCR. He
says that the numbers being helped by the Centre are falling,
not because the problem is diminishing, but because in the
past, when children were rescued, there was simply no one
to look after them. There were never enough staff with the
ability or resources to change the circumstances of the children, so they were sent back to the same situation in which
the abuse occurred.

*The idea now is to look for a comprehensive solution in
terms of our assessment of the case. Rehabilitation will not
be effective if it is not holistic. CPCR looks for what is
missing in the provision for children in Thailand and works
to fill that absence. We are not interested in taking over jobs
that belong to government agencies. We are not going to be
involved in investigations into pedophiles – we want the government to do that. In fact, more farang pedophiles than
brothel owners get arrested. It is easier to hit the customer.
Pedophiles fall into two categories – those who feel guilt and
remorse and those who don't. It is also important to deal
with child abuse in Western countries, because kids abused
there will be the abusers here in the future. The Crime
Suppression Division now deals with a lot of cases themselves. They tend to send the children to Public Welfare,
which is a corrective facility. The children come on to us if
the case is to go to court, because only we can prepare them
to testify. We would like to do more rehabilitation and this
work may expand as and when our resources permit.*

There are two rehabilitation houses close to the Centre.
These are in a pleasant residential district, in well-protected
compounds with gardens. Downstairs, there is a play space
for the children close to the workers' office, while the dormi-
tories are upstairs, bunk beds in a spacious open area. In one
bed, a young girl of about 12 is sleeping in the foetal position, thumb in her mouth, curled up against the world like a
flower against a cold wind. There are ten to twelve children
in each house at any one time, many of them with harrow-

ing stories. Rattiya Dalunsim is looking after the Tha Naam house, which is by the canal. We sit under the verandah outside, while inside some of the children play cards, talk with the workers, do their homework.

The rescued children come here to be rehabilitated, emotionally, physically, whatever is needed. Sometimes they go back to their family, sometimes not. Where sexual abuse has occurred in the family, we find other relatives to take care of them. In some cases, other charitable institutions provide a safe home. We have a staff of five here, a psychologist, a social worker and three other staff. The children stay on average three to six months, sometimes longer, depending on the case. There are few organisations that will take children on a long-term basis. It is better for them to go back to their native province if possible. The children here now are aged 5 to 18; mostly girls. There are only two boys.

When I visited two years before, there were a number of children who had been 'rescued' by a lawyer, who had in fact taken them into his house in order to abuse them. Rattiya says this case has been resolved. It did not go to court: two of the boys were returned to their families, two were taken by another organisation.

We have a boy here now who was physically abused. We rescued him in 1992. He is now seven years old. He was four when he first came. The mother had emotional problems. She had been divorced by the husband and the child remained with her. But she beat him and would not allow him to go outside the apartment. Maybe the mother could see in the boy something of the man who had deserted her. A citizen informed us, someone who had heard the child's persistent crying. At four years old, he could not speak, because she had never spoken to him. When he came here, his behaviour was erratic: when he got angry, he would hit and hurt himself, beat his head against the wall. Then he would beat the other children. He stayed one and a half years. We were able to control him, teach him the language. Then a psychiatrist saw the mother and child together. When he had improved, the mother came and took him away. When we visited after some time, his behaviour had regressed. So we took him once more. She comes to see him and when she does, she thinks she wants him with her; but she has so many problems of her own, she cannot see the needs of the child.

We had a girl who was raped by her own father. She was 14 years old. She had been sexually abused for four years. After she finished Grade VI, she came to Bangkok to look for a job. She had some medical problem and went to Chulalongkorn hospital. There, they noticed her behaviour was very silent and withdrawn. The psychiatrist spoke to her and then he informed us of the situation with her father. The girl came to stay with us. We visited the father and we wanted to make a case in the court. The mother was dead. We didn't know how she had died. We found out she had hanged herself. The father was a drinker and he quarrelled and fought with the family. She was here for one year. She was very sad. The father was arrested and jailed. She felt it was because of her and she punished herself: damaged herself and wouldn't communicate with anyone. The psychiatrist helped her to understand that it is not fitting for her father to do this to her. After counselling, we placed her in the care of another NGO, although we still keep good contact with her.

Often we are succesful and the children go back to their families. Sometimes the problems come back. We find that girls who have been abused for many years punish themselves, sometimes attempting to kill themselves. Other times, it is the family that is the problem. They think they can do as they like with their own children. This is a remainder of an older Thai culture, when people believed children were their own property. They think they have rights over them, but we say they also have duties and part of those duties is to respect the rights of the children.

Rattiya has been working in the rehabilitation centre for four years. Even in that short time, she has seen the problems change from child prostitution to sexual abuse within the family, which is now the main focus of the work. 'That doesn't mean child prostitution has stopped. But it changes its form. Before, the girls were placed in brothels and the police could raid them. Now they are in karaoke bars and cafés, places where it is not so easy to prove they are acting as prostitutes.' Rattiya was a teacher, a social worker, an office worker, and a company salesperson before she came here. She says she has never come across a female abuser in Thailand; but she does recognise that with consumerism has come a sexualising of the whole of society, especially in the interests of using sex in order to sell things to people.

This rehabilitation house, which has been rented to the Centre for 6000 baht a month (about 200 US dollars) for the past ten years, will be repossessed by the owner at the end of 1996. CPCR will never again get accommodation as spacious and as secure as this at such a low price. The work has in fact been subsidised by the owner; and when the tenancy runs out, the cost of the rehabilitation work will rise.

Chris Vertucci, of the End Child Prostitution in Asian Tourism (ECPAT) in Bangkok believes that the campaign must now extend its operations beyond the phenomenon of sex tourism to child pornography, trafficking in minors and the infrastructure that supports it. The whole commerce driving it must be targeted; and this will involve a wider critique, an understanding of some of the excesses of consumerism, in which a child can become another item of consumption, a holiday accessory. 'Everything now comes with a price tag on it and this is the mindset glorified by the global media.' Child prostitution is the product of a market economy that commodifies everything and glories in commodification. Several people in the Thai non-governmental organisations pointed out that the zeal with which the West is prepared to pursue child abusers is perhaps a symptom of their own guilt at some of the more unhappy consequences of its own creation, the market economy.

CONCLUSION

It might be possible to eliminate sex tourism, but it cannot
be done simply by targeting either the customers or the sex
workers. It is feasible, but extremely difficult, because the
struggle would have to be waged against a form of development that impoverishes vast numbers of people and leaves
them with little choice of occupation; while at the same
time, kindling some strange fantasies and 'needs' in those
who have the money and can travel half way round the
world to express them.

Siriporn Skrobanek throws the problem back to the West.
'In the West men do not marry or have long-term relationships with sex workers and nor do they expect to. Why then,
when they come here, do they look to marry? What mis-
perceptions permit them to think that Thai sex workers are
different from those in any other country? Even if they
declare that Thai women are in some way 'better', this is
still a racist projection because it does not recognise the
woman's reality. The sex tourism industry supplies a framework for these falsifications. The men are running away
from their own moral codes. They adopt a different one here,
in which they suspend the values they observe at home.'

Resistance to sex tourism, according to Siriporn and others,
should be part of a wider campaign against tourism in general;
and tourism is the largest single industry in the world in terms
of the money it generates. 'The ideology of cheap holidays is
part of the ideology of cheap goods, cheap labour and cheap
sex. In any case, you cannot even think of preventing people
from coming to Thailand for sex, because it would be impossible to distinguish them from other travellers. And many
people do develop long and enduring relationships sometimes

with women or men in the bars.' Siriporn Skrobanek thinks the best way to undermine the sex industry in Thailand is for the workers to become as efficient, indifferent and expensive as those in the West.

Even to attack child prostitution is less easy than it sounds. Sanphosit of the CPCR agrees with some of the workers at ECPAT, that even publishing details exposing pedophiles can simply supply others with information. There have been many newspaper articles, TV news items, magazine features on the theme. 'This can be counter-productive. We thought that to give the issue world-wide publicity would shame people. Yet we can see it may have the opposite effect.' One day when I was at the Centre for the Protection of Children's Rights, the workers were angry at a feature which the German magazine, *Stern*, had published and which had included many photographs of children which were themselves, in the opinion of Sanphosit, little better than soft porn pictures. Even the 'exposures' of wrongdoing come to have a startling double meaning.

In spite of these reservations, the general feeling among the NGOs is that campaigns against child sex tourism in the West are positive; at least, they deter 'opportunistic' abusers of children. But the West must examine its values and understand what creates the 'demand' for children. Similarly, Thailand must monitor and enforce existing legislation designed to protect children. Siriporn points out that, 'In the West, you do have official agencies which concern themselves with the rights and well-being of children. In Thailand there are laws, but these are not adequately enforced. They can be circumvented through corruption and the bribing of officials.'

Sanphosit quotes from US research into the relationship between child abusers and victims. 'If we understand this more fully, we may come to devise ways of bringing up boys which will protect them against becoming abusers. Ninety-nine per cent of clients in the sex trade are male. Boys are trained to be offenders and girls to be victims. To take good care of boys is vital, so they do not become hungry, predatory outcasts, the abusers of tomorrow.'

One of the greatest attractions of Thailand for people from the West rests on a profound cultural misapprehension between Thais and Westerners. This has to do with attitudes towards sex. Western society has been pan-sexualised in the past 50 years; that is to say, sex has become more and more explicit and more visible. It is used as a major element in advertising and selling all kinds of products which have nothing to do with sex. For many in the West, sexual experience comes to represent the most authentic of all human realities. This is reflected in the popular press and culture, the prurience with which the sex lives of the rich and famous are dissected and the prominence given to court reports of sexual wrongdoing. The search for the perfect orgasm, improved 'performance', sustained erection and pathways to greater pleasure suggest a search for transcendence through sex that may well simply not be available. 'This is not the case in Thailand. Sex is, naturally, important, but it is not invested with the same aura of mystic essentialism. In Thailand, it is more functional, matter-of-fact. Transcendence we reserve for religious experiences.'

The people in Thailand concerned with the sex industry offer some insight into why sex tourism has become both a problem and a challenge: the mismatch of perceptions between clients and sex workers; racism; dissatisfaction with Western constructs of sexuality and personhood; the socialisation of boys which turns them into aggressive, predatory men; the unequal status between clients and workers; and the uneven development between countries which confers such power on sex tourists. At the same time, the rapid industrialisation of Thailand, the mass migrations, scattering of traditional communities, the resistance of family support systems strained as never before, urbanisation and the degradation of the rural areas, drive people to the cities. These migrants have a quite different purpose in being there from the men who have come on vacation to take advantage of cheap sex, for extended leisure, to run away from failed relationships, or even as a gilded form of exile. It is inevitable that many of the encounters between these two vastly different and mutually uncomprehending worlds should so often result in breakdown, acrimony and unhappiness.

It is a savage irony that sex tourism should be one symptom of globalisation, the 'integration' of the whole world into a single economy, when both the workers in the industry and the clients from abroad are themselves the products of disintegration – of local communities, the dissolution of rootedness and belonging, the breaking of old patterns of labour and traditional livelihoods; and the psychic disintegration of so many people caught up in great epic changes, of which they have little understanding and over which they have less control.

APPENDIX

Useful contacts for those concerned with child sex tourism, and sex tourism in general.

END CHILD PROSTITUTION IN ASIAN TOURISM (ECPAT)
328 Phyathai Road, Bangkok 10400, Thailand.
Fax (66-2) 215-8272.

Established in Bangkok in 1991, by a community of concerned individuals and organisations to work together to end child prostitution in tourism. For the first three years it campaigned politically, for changes in the law, concentrating on education and media coverage. There are currently over 250 groups in the coalitions which form the ECPAT network in over 25 countries. ECPAT continues to campaign for action by governments in every country involved, to protect the rights of children. The governments of the Philippines, Sri Lanka, Taiwan, Thailand and Vietnam have all introduced stricter laws prohibiting child prostitution, even though the need for more effective law enforcement remains. Many rich countries are taking steps to change the legislation to facilitate the prosecution at home of their own nationals for offences committed against children overseas. In Norway, Sweden, Denmark, Finland, Iceland and Switzerland, extra-territoriality laws have existed for some time. More recently, legislation has been passed in Australia, Belgium, France, Germany, New Zealand and the USA, which holds their citizens accountable for offences committed against children abroad.

The second three-year phase of ECPAT's work builds on earlier achievements, and co-ordinates and monitors the developments, both in child sex tourism and resistance to it. The scope is broadening to include all children commercially exploited by the sex industry, trafficking, pornography and related issues.

COALITION ON CHILD PROSTITUTION
AND TOURISM
Co-ordinating Office,
Anti-Slavery International,
Unit 4, Stableyard, Broomgrove Road, London SW9 9TL.
Fax (+44) 738-4110.

This group is a coalition of NGOs – Anti-Slavery International, CAFOD, Christian Aid, Jubilee Campaign, Save the Children (UK), World Vision UK, National Society for the Prevention of Cruelty to Children, and War on Want. It was formed in March 1994 as a reaction to the report 'Wish You Weren't Here' commissioned by Save the Children Fund. The group's work has received widespread media coverage in the UK and has campaigned vigorously for extra-territorial legislation such as has been passed in many other Western countries, whereby their nationals may be prosecuted at home for offences committed abroad. The so-called Marshall Bill became law in 1996; it allows for the prosecution of tour operators but does not target individual travellers. The review of the legislation in July 1996 promises to include the extra-terrestrial provision which most other European countries have now passed. Anne Badger of the Coalition says, 'In any case, Britain will be among the last in Europe to pass such a law.'

EMPOWER, P.O. Box 1065, Silom P.O.
Bangkok 10504, Thailand.

EMPOWER was set up in Bangkok to work with women in the sex industry, to strengthen them against the bar owners, to teach them their legal rights, to help with health

APPENDIX   173

care and to give them greater negotiating power with their clients. This includes English-language teaching to enable them to communicate more effectively. Conditions for women working in the international sex industry have improved – many can now refuse clients who refuse to use a condom – although they are still exploited, both by owners and customers. EMPOWER has extended its work now to the suburban areas of Bangkok, where conditions have, if anything, worsened for women and girls who live in semi-captivity in some of the closed brothels patronised mainly by Thai men.

FOUNDATION FOR WOMEN
P.O. Box 47, Bangkoknoi, Bangkok 10700, Thailand.

FOUNDATION FOR WOMEN campaigns on behalf of women in Thailand and has recently initiated a vigorous dialogue with all parties concerned in the sex industry. There has been much advocacy work on behalf of Thai women trafficked to other parts of the world, Japan, Europe, Australia, the USA and employed, often against their will, as entertainers and prostitutes in those countries. In particular, current work concentrates on the trafficking in young women and girls, especially from the hill tribes of Northern Thailand, from Burma, Yunnan province in southern China, Laos and Cambodia.

FRIENDS OF WOMEN
1379/30, Soi Praditchai,
Samsennai Phayati, Paholyothin Road,
Bangkok 10400, Thailand.

FRIENDS OF WOMEN is working on alternative employment to the sex industry. There is an emphasis on inducing young women not to migrate to the city and providing livelihood in the rural areas. This NGO also offers legal advice to individual women in cases of exploitation at work, marriage law, human rights, as well as all areas of violence against women.

TASK FORCE TO FIGHT AGAINST
CHILD EXPLOITATION (FACE)
c/o Office of International Affairs, Rangsit University,
Muang-Ake, Paholyathin Road, Pathumthai, Thailand.

This is a high-powered organisation directly concerned with
all areas of exploitation of children in South Asia.

FOUNDATION FOR RURAL YOUTH
90/61 Senanikom Lane, Paholyathin Road, Ladprao,
Bangkok 10230, Thailand.

This group is working with young people in industry, many
of them new migrants to Bangkok. It aims to protect them
and their interests in exploitative work situations. It also
works in villages in Isan in the Northeast of Thailand and
ideally, would wish to see rural-urban migration reduced. In
the absence of changing macro policies, the group concentrates on preparing newcomers to Bangkok to help them
understand the kind of life they may expect and to
strengthen them so they may resist falling into prostitution
and the worst kinds of exploitative labour.

THAI RED CROSS PROGRAM ON AIDS
Red Cross Society, 1871 Rama IV Road,
Bangkok 10330, Thailand.

Research and prevention work among sex workers, in the gay
community and among migrant workers.

CENTRE FOR THE PROTECTION
OF CHILDREN'S RIGHTS (CPCR)
185/16 Soi Wat Dee Duat, Cahransanitwong 12 Rd,
Bangkok Yai, Bangkok 10600, Thailand.
Fax (+66–2) 412–9833)

This has been a pioneering organisation which has led campaigns against the abuse and exploitation of children for 15

years. It undertakes investigations and rescue operations for
young people aged under 18, whose basic human rights have
been violated. It offers protection, temporary shelter, social
welfare support, holistic rehabilitation and legal advocacy.
Having crusaded against overwork of children in factories, it
moved on to abuse – punitive and sexual – within the family, as well as with sexually abused and prostituted children.
CPCR has taken up child protection issues that have not
been addressed by other Thai organisations and works with a
wide network of government departments and other NGOs.

WAR ON WANT

A UK campaigning charity which works in partnership with
oppressed people world-wide, is dedicated to fighting all
forms of discrimination and recognises that in working to
defend one another's rights we work to defend our own.
Among recent initiatives has been a campaign for the human
right to development, which means the right to subsistence
and security for all on earth. WAR ON WANT is working with
organisations protecting lesbians and gay men in countries
which criminalise and oppress them. WAR ON WANT has
joined the Coalition on Child Prostitution and Tourism and
is campaigning in partnership with women and children
whose rights are violated by sex tourism.